The Birth-mark

to-day and to-morrow, and the
day following: for it cannot be
that a prophet perish out of Jerusalem.
34 O Jerusalem, Jerusalem,
which killest the prophets, and
stonest them that are sent unto
thee; how often would I have
gathered thy children together,
as a hen *doth gather* her brood
under *her* wings, and ye would
not!
35 Behold, your house is left
unto you desolate. And verily, I
say unto you, Ye shall not see
me, until *the time* come when ye
shall say, Blessed *is* he that
cometh in the name of the
Lord.

Herman Melville's penciled marginal annotations in his copy of *The Authorized New Testament with Psalms* (New York: American Bible Society, 1844). The passages are from Luke 13. (By permission of the Houghton Library, Harvard University.)

THE BIRTH-MARK

unsettling the wilderness in American literary history

Susan Howe

Wesleyan University Press
Published by University Press of New England
Hanover and London

Wesleyan University Press
Published by University Press of New England,
Hanover, NH 03755

Printed in the United States of America
5 4 3 2 1
CIP data appear at the end of the book
Permission acknowledgments appear on page 191

In the centre of Georgiana's left cheek, there was a singular mark, deeply interwoven, as it were, with the texture and substance of her face. In the usual state of her complexion,—a healthy, though delicate bloom,—the mark wore a tint of deeper crimson, which imperfectly defined its shape amid the surrounding rosiness. When she blushed, it gradually became more indistinct, and finally vanished amid the triumphant rush of blood, that bathed the whole cheek with its brilliant glow. But, if any shifting emotion caused her to turn pale, there was the mark again, a crimson stain upon the snow, in what Aylmer sometimes deemed an almost fearful distinctness. Its shape bore not a little similarity to the human hand, though of the smallest pigmy size.

—Nathaniel Hawthorne, "The Birth-mark"

```
Vesuvius  dont  talk  - Etna .dont -
They  said a  syllable  one of them
a  thousand  years  ago , and
Pompeii  heard  it ,  and  hid
forever - She  couldnt  look the
world  in  the  face , afterward -
I suppose -   Bashful Pompeii !
"Tell you  of  the  want - you
know  what  a  leech  is , dont
           remember that
you - and  Daisys  arm   is small -
```

—Emily Dickinson, "Third Master Letter"

Though our Handsome Sailor had as much of masculine beauty as one can expect anywhere to see; nevertheless, like the beautiful woman in one of Hawthorne's minor tales, there was just one thing amiss in him. No visible blemish indeed, as with the lady; no, but an occasional liability to a vocal defect. Though in the hour of elemental uproar or peril he was everything that a sailor should be, yet under sudden provocation of strong heart-feeling his voice, otherwise singularly musical, as if expressive of the harmony within, was apt to develop an organic hesitancy, in fact more or less of a stutter or even worse.

—Herman Melville, *Billy-Budd*

Contents

Acknowledgments

Patricia Caldwell's *The Puritan Conversion Narrative: The Beginnings of American Expression* and Charles Lloyd Cohen's *God's Caress: The Psychology of Puritan Religious Experience* examine, in different ways, a body of materials not featured in our American literary canon. The texts they examine are testimonies, delivered by men and women, in the gathered Nonconformist churches of England, Ireland, and New England between the 1630s and the Restoration. Few of these religious narratives have survived. On the American side, the most interesting collection is a group of fifty-one recorded in a small private notebook by Thomas Shepard, the minister of the First Church in Cambridge, Massachusetts, between 1637 and 1645, either as they were being delivered or shortly afterward from notes and memory. The first complete edition of these narratives, edited by George Selement and Bruce C. Woolley, was published in volume 58 of *Collections of the Colonial Society of Massachusetts* in 1981. Some of these confessions of faith had previously appeared in other anthologies, but none of those given by women. Apart from the court records of Anne Hutchinson's trials and a few brief "relations" in John Fiske's and Michael Wigglesworth's notebooks, these testimonies represent the first voices of English women speaking in New England. As in Anne Hutchinson's case their words were transcribed by male mediators who were also community leaders. *The Puritan Conversion Narrative* demonstrates how careful examination and interpretation of individual physical artifacts from a time and place can change our basic assumptions about the New England pattern and its influence on American literary expression.

Caldwell's study is concerned with how and when English voices began speaking New-Englandly. In her essay "The Antinomian Language Controversy" (*Harvard Theological Review* 69 [1976] pp. 345–67), Caldwell writes: "trial documents suggest that Mrs. Hutchinson was neither purposely deceiving nor hallucinating, and that her words cannot fairly be ascribed to mere stubbornness, hysteria, and personal assertiveness, nor even to a poor education. They suggest that Mrs. Hutchinson was speaking what amounts to a different language—different from that of her adversaries, different even from that of John Cotton—and that other people may have been speaking and hearing as she was, and that what happened to them all had serious literary consequences in America" (pp. 346–47). This antinomian language occurred again in the controversial years before, during, and immediately after the American Civil War. Michael Colacurcio and Amy Shrager Lang have shown that Hawthorne's short stories and *The Scarlet Letter* are inspired and unsettled by Mrs. Hutchinson's role as a prophetic religious leader.

Amy Shrager Lang's *Prophetic Woman: Anne Hutchinson and the Problem of Dissent in the Literature of New England* demonstrates that American antinomianism is a separate phenomenon from its European counterpart. Here, the history of antinomianism in the Massachusetts Bay Colony (1635–37), encoded in the story of Anne Hutchinson, is gendered from the beginning. Lang's thesis that the local history of antinomianism is distinct from its universal one was supplanted for me by Anne Kibbey's invaluable chapter, "1637: The Pequot War and the Antinomian Controversy," in *The Interpretation of Material Shapes in Puritanism*, a book to which I return again and again, and by Stephen Greenblatt's "The Word of God in the Age of Mechanical Reproduction" in his *Renaissance Self-Fashioning: From More to Shakespeare*. This essay has been important to my thinking about sixteenth- and seventeenth-century English Protestant biblical translators, prophets, and heretics.

My work on Mary Rowlandson was originally inspired and explicitly aided by Richard Slotkin's *Regeneration through Violence: The Mythology of the American Frontier, 1600–1860*. Julia Kristeva's "Semiotics of Biblical Abomination," in *Powers of Horror: An Essay on Abjection*, was helpful for a reading of Rowlandson's narrative. *Cotton Mather and Benjamin Franklin: The Price of Representative Personality*, by Mitchell Robert Breitwieser, and Kenneth Silverman's *The Life and Times of Cotton Mather* contributed to my understanding of Cotton Mather. *God's Plot: The Paradoxes of Puritan Piety, Being the Autobiography & Journal of Thomas Shepard*, edited and with an illuminating introduction by Michael McGiffert, brings Shepard alive as no other writing about him has done. The Selement and Woolley edition of Shepard's *Confessions* have been indispensable, not least for the genealogical records they so painstakingly supplied for each speaker. I have, in "Incloser," retained the names Shepard used as headings for his narratives; the section on beaver dams in this essay draws on William Cronon's *Changes in the Land: Indians, Colonists, and the Ecology of New England*, a book I also found useful in more general ways in my Rowlandson essay. Although my reading of American literary expression is bleaker than readings offered by Sacvan Bercovitch, I have profited from his reassessments of the Puritan errand.

When I started "Incloser," I used *Webster's Third New International Dictionary* as the source for a definition of *enclosure*. Since then I have come to believe that what is crucial when trying to understand what makes the literary expression of Emerson, Thoreau, Melville, Dickinson, and to a lesser extent Hawthorne singularly North American is their use—and in Dickinson's case, intentional misuse—of Noah Webster's original *American Dictionary of the English Language* (1828). The Dickinson family owned a copy of the first edition, and Webster, who for a time lived in Amherst, was a family friend. Emily Dickinson herself owned an 1844 reprint of the Webster's updated 1840 edition.

The full title of the 1828 edition reads: *An American dictionary of the English language: intended to exhibit, I. The origin, affinities and primary signification of English words, as far as they have been ascertained. II. The genuine orthography and pronunciation of words, according to general usage, or to just principles of analogy. III. Accurate and discriminating definitions, with numerous authorities and illustrations. To which are prefixed, an introductory dissertation on the origin, history and connection of the languages of Western Asia and of Europe, and a concise grammar of the English language*: a title worthy of Cotton Mather. *Enclosure*, Noah Webster insists here, should begin with an *i*.

* * *

Until the English Department at SUNY Buffalo gave me a one-semester appointment as Butler Chair Professor of English in 1989, I had no academic affiliation. The seminar I taught there facilitated my research. Later, an appointment as Writer in Residence at Temple University put me in touch with Rachel Blau DuPlessis, Toby Olson, Lawrence Venuti and Susan Stewart, all of whom encouraged me in the writing of these essays. Three other scholars, two in the field of textual scholarship and the other an Early Americanist, encouraged me during this time. Jerome McGann's interest in the problems of editing Dickinson's manuscripts has given me the courage to keep exploring their implications. Ulla Dydo, who is currently working on the problems of editing Gertrude Stein's writing, has also encouraged my ventures into textual scholarship. Janice Knight discussed the Shepard essay with me and contributed her critical insight. Marjorie Perloff and Charles Bernstein have helped me in countless ways. My thanks to Peter Quartermain for his invaluable final critique of the manuscript and for his editorial suggestions during the time I was writing the Introduction/ Submarginalia section. Robert Creeley's essays on American writing have been a model for me. Donald H. Reiman (with the Bodleian Library's permission) was kind enough to allow me to use material from the Garland edition of the *Bodleian Shelley Manuscripts*. I thank the New England Historical and Genealogical Society for allowing me to examine Shepard's manuscript book containing the "Confessions," the Houghton Library at Harvard University for allowing me to study Shepard's manuscript book containing "T• {My Birth & Life} S," as well as Herman Melville's marked copies of *Twice-told Tales*, *Mosses from an Old Manse*, *Shelley Memorials*, and Southey's *Life of Nelson* among others of his books. I am grateful to Rodney Dennis for giving me permission to examine two of Dickinson's original manuscript books, also owned by Houghton Library. I would like to have seen more of them.

An early draft of the essay on Mary Rowlandson was originally presented as part of three lectures on Emily Dickinson I gave at New College in San Francisco, 1984. Another draft was presented at the New Poetics Colloquium of the Kootenay School of Writing at the Emily Carr College of Art and Design, Vancouver, British Columbia, August 1985. Parts of "The Captivity and Restoration of Mrs. Mary Rowlandson" were published in *Temblor* 2 (1985). An early draft of "Incloser" was presented as a talk for a series curated by Charles Bernstein at the Wolfson Center for National Affairs of the New School for Social Research, Fall 1988. Some of "Incloser" was published in *The Politics of Poetic Form: Poetry and Public Policy*, edited by Charles Bernstein, Roof Books, 1990, and in *Postmodern Culture* 1.2 (January 1991); some of it was published as a fine press edition by Weaselsleeves Press, Santa Fe, New Mexico, 1992.

"These Flames and Generosities of the Heart" was published in *Sulfur* 27 (Spring 1991). Some of it was part of a slide lecture called "The Illogic of Sumptuary Values" that I delivered first at an Emily Dickinson—H.D. Dual Centennial Colloquium at San Jose State University in October 1986. Portions from that lecture were published in *How(ever)* magazine (vol. 3, no. 4, 1987).

Edward Foster's interview was published in *Talisman: A Journal of Contemporary Prose and Poetics*, no. 4 (Spring 1990).

Elizabeth Willis, Marta Werner, Mark von Schlegell, Mike Cartmell and Benjamin Friedlander assisted me in preparing the final manuscript. I am very lucky to have had Jim Schley as the copy editor for this eccentric textual production.

Marta Werner's careful and courageous rereading of Emily Dickinson's writing is always an inspiration.

Most of all, I thank David von Schlegell for the example, beside me for twenty-seven years, of one person's lifelong dedication to art and for his belief in "creation as content" as it is reflected in his sculpture and painting.

Guilford, Connecticut S. H.
August 1992

The Birth-mark

Introduction

These essays were written after *My Emily Dickinson.* They are the direct and indirect results of my encounter with *The Manuscript Books of Emily Dickinson*, edited by R. W. Franklin for the Belknap Press of Harvard University Press in 1981, and with *The Master Letters of Emily Dickinson*, also edited by R. W. Franklin, this time for the Amherst College Press in 1986. There I learned, examining the facsimiles, that Emily Dickinson, in her carefully handwritten manuscripts—some sewn into fascicles, some gathered into sets—may have been demonstrating her conscious and unconscious separation from a mainstream literary orthodoxy in letters, an orthodoxy not only represented by T. W. Higginson's and Mabel Loomis Todd's famous editorial interference but also to be found during the 1950s in Thomas H. Johnson's formal assumptions—assumptions apparently shared by Ralph Franklin (if one is to judge by the "Introduction" to *The Master Letters*). The issue of editorial control is directly connected to the attempted erasure of antinomianism in our culture. Lawlessness seen as negligence is at first feminized and then restricted or banished. For me, the manuscripts of Emily Dickinson represent a contradiction to canonical social power, whose predominant purpose seems to have been to render isolate voices devoted to writing as a physical event of immediate revelation. The excommunication and banishment of the early American female preacher and prophet Anne Hutchinson, and the comparison of her opinions to monstrous births, is not unrelated to the editorial apprehension and domestication of Emily Dickinson. The antinomian controversy in New England (1636–38) didn't leave Massachusetts with its banished originator. The antinomian controversy continues in the form, often called formlessness, of Dickinson's letters and poems during and after her crisis years of 1858–60. It continues with this nineteenth-century antinomian poet's gesture of infinite patience in preferring not to publish. Her demurral was a covenant of grace. The antinomian controversy continues in the first reordering and revision of her manuscripts according to a covenant of works. The antinomian controversy continues in the manhandling of the Thomas H. Johnson editions of *The Poems of Emily Dickinson: Including Variant Readings Critically Compared with All Known Manuscripts* (1951) and *The Letters of Emily Dickinson* (1958), published by the Belknap Press of Harvard University Press. It continues in the current magisterial control of her copyrights and access to her papers exercised by the Houghton Library at Harvard University, the Harvard University Press, and to a lesser degree the Amherst College Library and the Amherst College Press. In July 1862, Emily Dickinson prophetically wrote to T. W. Higginson: "if at any time—you regret you received me, or I prove a different fabric to that you supposed—you must banish me—" (L 268).

Emily Dickinson's writing is my strength and shelter. I have trespassed into the disciplines of American Studies and Textual Criticism through my need to fathom what wildness and absolute freedom is the nature of expression. There are other characteristic North American voices and visions that remain antinomian and separatist. In order to hear them I have returned by strange paths to a particular place at a particular time, a threshold at the austere reach of the book.

* * *

Is there a poem that never reaches words

And one that chaffers the time away?
Is the poem peculiar and general?
There's a meditation there, in which there seems

To be an evasion, a thing not apprehended or
Not apprehended well. Does the poet
evade us, as in a senseless element?

Wallace Stevens, "Notes toward a Supreme Fiction" (TS 135)

First: before political theory people have no property. First: before civil order the arm of the church must extend its reach. First: the Law holds gibberish off. Follow the footprints of justices.

Here are unmown fields unknown inhabitants other woods in other words: enigma of gibberish unwritten wife

Poetry unsettles our scrawled defence; unapprehensible but dear nevertheless.

"and behold / the academies like structures in a mist." (TS 124)

* * *

When a group of English Puritans entered into an explicit contract they called a Covenant with God and left the European continent in what later came to be known as the Great Migration of the 1630s, they were trespassers. Although these colonists were propelled by a desire to escape religious and economic constraints, they were also anxious not to be considered Separatist. Circumstances they could not have foreseen enjoined a particular separatism. America as Educator. Here there was nothing to withdraw from but forsakenness.

First: these separating nonSeparatists were lawless in their particular northwestern settlement abroad in the world at the eastern margin of a continent. But a utopian exodus can't allow negligence. Humanity imposes obligations. The "Absolute Boundary of Reformation" is too immediately unsettling. As if speech must always recall sensation to order, the covenantal dialect installed its particular violences; its singular body and monologue of command expressions. Seventy years later, Cotton Mather's "A General Introduction" to the *Magnalia Christi Americana: or, The Ecclesiastical History of New-England, from Its First Planting in the Year 1620, unto the Year of Our* LORD, *1698, in Seven* BOOKS, nervously assures the reader: "But whether *New England* may *Live* any where else or no, it must *Live* in our *History*!" (MC 94).

One of the vivid "Lives of Sixty Famous Divines" in *Magnalia Christi Americana* is titled "Cottonus Redivivus; or, The Life of Mr. John Cotton." John Cotton, the historian Cotton Mather's maternal grandfather, was a library cormorant. "Mr. Cotton was indeed a most *universal scholar*, and a *living system* of the liberal arts, and a *walking library*. . . . Twelve hours in a day he commonly studied, and would call that *a scholar's day*; resolving rather to wear out with using than with rusting" (MC 273–76). John Cotton was also Anne Hutchinson's minister, friend, and eventually persecutor. Sometime during the antinomian controversy in New England a spark from the fire of Scripture singed the heart of the minister-scholar. "If we be hemm'd in with this Covenant we cannot break out," he once wrote.

America as Educator.

During its turbulent infancy, discourse in the Massachusetts Bay Colony, religious or otherwise, stirred by millenarian activism, fraught with puzzlement and rapture, fury and passivity, was charged with particular risks for women, who were hedged in by a network of old-world property values. *Charged*: "But now having seen him which is invisible I fear not what man can do unto me" (AC 338), said Mrs. Anne Hutchinson at her Examination at the Court at Newtowne/Cambridge. The antinomian controversy was the primordial struggle of North American literary expression. The real Anne Hutchinson was banished by the founders of the Massachusetts Bay Colony, then murdered in the natural wilderness by history. Emily Dickinson's textual production is still being tamed for aesthetic consumption. If antinomian vision in North America is gendered feminine, then what will save it from print misfortune?

* * *

"

Voices I am following lead me to the margins. Anne Hutchinson's verbal expression is barely audible in the scanty second- or thirdhand records of her two trials. Dorothy Talbye, Mrs. Hopkins, Mary Dyer, Thomas Shepard, Mrs. Sparhawk, Brother Crackbone's wife, Mary Rowlandson, Barbary Cutter, Cotton Mather may have been searching for grace in the wilderness of the world. They express to me a sense of unrevealedness. They walk in my imagination and I love them. Somewhere Coleridge says that Love may be a sense of Substance/Being seeking to be self-conscious

you. Fate flies home to the mark. Can any words restore to me how you *felt*?

you are straying, seeking, scattering. Was it you or is it me? Where is the stumbling block? Thoughts delivered by love are predestined to distortion by words. If experience forges conception, can quick particularities of caligraphic expression ever be converted to type? Are words children? What is the exchange value? Where does spirit go? Double yourself stammer stammer. Is there any way to proof it? Who or what survives the work? Where is the patron of the stamp?

Mosses Moses Moby muffled maybe

I am drawn toward the disciplines of history and literary criticism but in the dawning distance a dark wall of rule supports the structure of every letter, record, transcript: every proof of authority and power. I know records are compiled by winners, and scholarship is in collusion with Civil Government. I know this and go on searching for some trace of love's infolding through all the paper in all the libraries I come to.

* * *

Old News

For a time, Nathaniel Hawthorne was a cormorant of libraries. After graduation from Bowdoin College in 1825 he returned to his mother's home in Salem. For most of the next ten years he lived with his mother, two sisters, a maternal uncle, and probably two aunts. There seems to have been little pressure on him to earn an income, and he was left alone to write. Between 1826 and 1838 his sister Elizabeth (another library cormorant) borrowed over a thousand books for her brother and herself, usually from the Salem Athenaeum. "The Athenaeum was very defective," Elizabeth later recalled, "it was one of my brother's peculiarities that he would never visit it himself, nor look over the Catalogue to select a book, nor do anything indeed but find fault with it; so that it was left entirely to me to provide him with reading, and I'm sure nobody else would have got half so much out of such a dreary old library as I did. . . . 6 vols. folio, of Howell's State Trials, he preferred to any others. There was also much that related to the early history of New England, with which I think he became pretty well acquainted, aided, no doubt, by the Puritan instinct that was in him" (EH 324). Michael Colacurcio thinks Hawthorne may have felt many of his stories were ironic repetitions of already familiar ones, and this is why he called the first book he signed his name to *Twice-told Tales*. Hawthorne's most recent biographer, Edwin Haviland Miller, thinks he simply meant these stories, now in book form, had already been published in magazines. The title could also be a reference to lines in Shakespeare's *King John*: "Life is as tedious as a twice-told tale, / Vexing the dull ear of a drowsy man." Coincidentally or uncannily, *Twice-told Tales* was published in 1837, exactly two hundred years after the antinomian controversy. In 1837, Sara Coleridge's long fairy tale, "Phantasmion," was published in England. "It requires no great *face* to publish nowadays; it is not stepping upon a stage where the eyes of an audience are upon you—but entering a crowd, where you must be very tall, strong, and striking, indeed, to obtain the slightest attention. In these days, too, to print a Fairy Tale is the very way to be *not read*, but shoved aside with contempt," she wrote in a letter to a friend (SD 95).

* * *

In 1851, while he was rewriting *Moby-Dick*, Herman Melville, another library cormorant, marked a passage in his copy of Hawthorne's story "The Gentle Boy." " 'Friend,' replied the little boy, in a sweet, though faultering voice, 'they call me Ilbrahim, and my home is here' " (H 111). "The Gentle Boy" is one of Hawthorne's *Twice-told Tales*, although he wrote it years earlier and published it first, anonymously, in a magazine. Quaker antinomian Catherine is Ilbrahim's mother. She erupts into the narrative, as the muffled essence of enthusiasm.

> The muffled female, who had hitherto sat motionless in the front rank of the audience, now arose, and with slow, stately, and unwavering step, ascended the pulpit stairs. . . . She then divested herself of the cloak and hood, and appeared in a most singular array. A shapeless robe of sackcloth was girded about her waist with a knotted cord; her raven hair fell down upon her shoulders, and its blackness was defiled by pale streaks of ashes, which she had strewn upon her head. Her eyebrows, dark and strongly defined, added to the deathly whiteness of a countenance, which, emaciated with want, and wild with enthusiasm and strange sorrows, retained no trace of earlier beauty. (H 118)

Antinomian Anne Hutchinson roams through Nathaniel Hawthorne's imagination in *The Scarlet Letter*. After the introductory custom-house chapter she is immediately there at the prison door.

> This rose-bush, by a strange chance, has been kept alive in history; but whether it had merely survived out of the stern old wilderness, so long after the fall of the gigantic pines and oaks that overshadowed it,—or whether, as there is fair authority for believing, it had sprung up under the footsteps of the sainted Ann Hutchinson, as she entered the prison-door,—we shall not take upon us to determine. Finding it so directly on the threshold of our narrative, which is now about to issue from that inauspicious portal, we could hardly do otherwise than pluck one of its flowers and present it to the reader. (SL 50)

The Scarlet Letter: A Romance is fiction. "The Birth-mark" is the first story in Nathaniel Hawthorne's collection of short stories *Mosses from an Old Manse*. Herman Melville called his essay on Hawthorne and American literary expression "Hawthorne and His Mosses." "The Birth-mark" is a twice-told title.

* * *

The Public Eye

Noah Webster defines *edit* this way: "1. *Properly*, to publish; *more usually*, to superintend a publication; to prepare a book or paper for the public eye, by writing, correcting, or selecting the matter."

> One day, very soon after their marriage, Aylmer sat gazing at his wife, with a trouble in his countenance that grew stronger, until he spoke.
>
> "Georgiana," said he, "has it never occured to you that the mark upon your cheek might be removed?"
>
> "No, indeed," said she, smiling; but perceiving the seriousness of his manner, she blushed deeply. "To tell you the truth, it has been so often called a charm, that I was simple enough to imagine it might be so."
>
> "Ah, upon another face, perhaps it might," replied her husband. "But never on yours! No, dearest Georgiana, you came so nearly perfect from the hand of Nature, that this slightest possible defect—which we hesitate whether to term a defect or a beauty—shocks me, as being the visible mark of earthly imperfection." (H 764–65)

In 1844, Edgar Allan Poe wrote several introductory passages concerning what he called his "idle practice" of making notes in the margins of books. He called the introduction and "subjoined *farrago*" "Marginalia." This was the first of a group of pieces he contributed under the same title to the *Democratic Review, Graham's, Godey's* magazines and the *Southern Literary Messenger* over the next five years.

> In the *marginalia* . . . we talk only to ourselves; we therefore talk freshly—boldly—originally—with *abandonnement*—without conceit—much after the fashion of Jeremey Taylor, and Sir Thomas Browne, and Sir William Temple, and the anatomical Burton, and that most logical analogist, Butler, and some other people of the old day, who were too full of their matter to have any room for their manner, which, being thus left out of the question, was a capital manner, indeed,—a model of manners, with a richly marginalic air. . . . It may be as well to observe . . . that just as the goodness of your true pun is in the direct ratio of its intolerability, so is nonsense the essential sense of the Marginal Note. (PW 1–4)

* * *

Marginalia

When Hawthorne was an undergraduate at Bowdoin College (1821–25), one of his nicknames was Oberon. "Oh! I have a horror of what was created in my own brain, and shudder at the manuscripts in which I gave that dark idea a sort of material existence. Would they were out of my sight" (H 331), exclaims the author's fictional author Oberon in "The Devil in Manuscript," before he burns his stories. "The Devil in Manuscript," an early tale, was published anonymously in 1835. "The papers were indeed reduced to a heap of black cinders, with a multitude of sparks hurrying confusedly among them, the traces of the pen being now represented by white lines, and the whole mass fluttering two and fro, in the draughts of air" (H 335). In 1842, Edgar Allan Poe wrote a review of *Twice-told Tales* for *Graham's Magazine*; he advised Hawthorne to "mend his pen, get a bottle of visible ink, come out from the old Manse, cut Mr. Alcott, hang (if possible) the editor of 'The Dial,' and throw out of the window to the pigs all his odd numbers of 'The North American Review' " (PS 450).

"—Of Poe, I know too little to think—Hawthorne appalls, entices—." In 1879, Emily Dickinson was thanking T. W. Higginson for the Christmas present of his recently published *Short Studies of American Authors*. Higginson's book contained critical sketches of Hawthorne, Poe, Thoreau, Howells, Helen Hunt Jackson, and Henry James. The author of possibly a thousand unpublished poems sagely added, "Mrs Jackson soars to your estimate lawfully as a Bird, but of Howells and James, one hesitates—Your relentless music dooms as it redeems—" (L 622).

Editing is the art of discipline; the mastery of detail. Eccentric punctuation, blots, dashes, smudged letters, gaps, interruptions, aborted sketches, "textually irrelevant" numbers, uncanceled or canceled alternatives in the manuscript are a profitless counteraction. Editing is sensible partitioning.

The contents page of Melville's edition of *Mosses from an Old Manse* has a printer's error. "Egotism, or; the Bosom-Friend, FROM THE UNPUBLISHED 'ALLEGORIES OF THE HEART'" should read "Egotism, or, the Bosom-Serpent." Melville corrected the misprint by drawing a line through the word "friend" and writing "serpent" above it (MM 1:619).

" 'Here he comes!' shouted the boys along the street.—'Here comes the man with a snake in his bosom!' " (H 781) is the beginning of "Egotism."

"So much for the intellect! But where was the heart?" (H 1051) wonders Hawthorne's transgressive investigator Ethan Brand shortly before throwing himself into the furnace of a lime kiln on Mount Graylock. When Hawthorne published "Ethan Brand" in 1850, he had already written *Twice-told Tales* and *Mosses*.

In spite of the zealous searching of editors, authors, and publishers for the print-perfect proof of intellectual labor, the heart may be sheltering in some random mark of communication. Cancelations, variants, insertions, erasures, marginal notes, stray marks and blanks in John Winthrop's manuscript notebooks are neither a "Journal" nor a "History." Maybe they are memories in disguise. Thomas Shepard's inky Elizabethan embellishments emblazon many of his confessors' names. The Puritan minister's shorthand pen strokes, vertical dashes, abbreviations, and lists in another manuscript book may be a mimic autobiography or a counter-character and career. "When my brother was young, he covered the margins and the fly leafs of every book in the house with lines of poetry and other quotations, and with his own name, and other names. Nothing brings him back to me so vividly as looking at those old books" (EH 331), Elizabeth Hawthorne recalled to James T. Fields in 1871 when he was collecting information for his biography of Hawthorne. The marginal marks Herman Melville made in his copy of Hawthorne's *Mosses from an Old Manse* are another kind of writing, as are Dickinson's word variants, directional dashes and crosses. Editors too often remove these original marks of "imperfection" or muffle them in appendixes and prefaces.

"Then why did you take me from my mother's side? You cannot love what shocks you!" cries fictional Georgiana in the "The Birth-mark" (H 765). Hawthorne wrote it over two hundred years after the real Anne Hutchinson was excommunicated and banished by an affiliation of ministers and magistrates for the crime of religious enthusiasm. The original records of her two trials have been lost. In 1830, "Mrs. Hutchinson" was one of Hawthorne's first published stories. He removed it from later collections gathered into books. The nervous author went to great lengths to destroy his first novel, *Fanshawe*, published anonymously at his own expense in 1828. Not only did he burn the manuscript, but he did everything possible to eradicate the few existing copies. Hawthorne persuaded his closest friend, Horatio Bridge, to destroy his edition of the book and never mention it to anyone. He concealed *Fanshawe*'s existence from his wife, who didn't know he had written it until after his death.

George is the first name of the first president of the United States. George Washington always tells the truth goes our primal myth.

"But the deeper went the knife, the deeper sank the Hand, until at length its tiny grasp appeared to have caught hold of Georgiana's heart; whence, however, her husband was inexorably resolved to cut or wrench it away" (H 767). Every lie leads deep into itself.

The intuitive retrospection of Hawthorne's unpremeditated art is just beyond the genealogy of civil reach. Ann's name holds on.

* * *

Under the Banner of Young America

"Where do we find ourselves?" is the opening question of Emerson's essay "Experience." "Words! book-words! what are you?" asks the Poet in Whitman's "Song of the Banner at Daybreak." "For what are we, mere strips of cloth profiting nothing, / Only flapping in the wind?" the Banner and Pennant ask back. "I use the wings of the land-bird and use the wings of the sea-bird, and look down as from a height," the Poet replies (LG 241). F. O. Matthiessen used the Whitman quotation in *American Renaissance: Art and Expression in the Age of Emerson and Whitman* as an epigraph to the chapter called "Only a Language Experiment."

"O you up there! O pennant! where you undulate like a snake hissing so curious, / Out of reach, an idea only, yet furiously fought for, risking bloody death, loved by me, / So loved—" (LG 244).

* * *

An Idea of Enthusiasm

In January 1939, F. O. Matthiessen wrote a letter to himself while he was a patient at McLean Hospital. At the time the Harvard professor, cultural historian, scholar, critic, and library cormorant was writing the book that became the classic text for American studies until the revisionary 1960s and 1970s. Matthiessen entered the hospital when suffering from depression, anxiety, and worry over his inability to finish the work; he was recurrently overwhelmed with the desire to kill himself by jumping from a window.

> Why? That is what is so baffling, so unfathomed. Because my talent was less than I thought? Because, on the first onset, I couldn't write the book I wanted? Such reasons seem preposterous to anyone reasonable, and certainly they do to me. . . . For even though it should

> turn out that I am an enthusiast trying to be a critic, a Platonic rhapsode trying to be an Aristotelian, that means a fairly hard period of readjustment, but scarcely grounds for death for a man of thirty-six. But what if you found out you couldn't write any book at all? But why introduce that phantom when you have already written three? Must it be aut Caesar aut nullus? Must everything meet you on your first terms? As Dr. Barret said a couple of days ago, "No one kills himself over a book." And I answered, "Nobody but a goddamned fool, and I'm not a goddamned fool."
>
> Towards the end of my session with Dr. Fremont-Smith he dwelt on the danger of fear, and perhaps intuitively introduced the fear of the death of someone you loved. . . . Bruno [Kollar] once remarked on how conscious I was. The American mind terribly aware of itself. Has its bright scrutiny, the self-knowledge which I have believed to be my sureness in making my life an integrated one, shut off more than I am aware, has it left nine-tenths of the ice-berg hidden? (RD 245–47)

An antinomian is a religious enthusiast. Noah Webster defines an enthusiast as "1. One who imagines he has special or supernatural converse with God, or special communications from him. 2. One whose imagination is warmed, one whose mind is highly excited with the love or in the pursuit of an object; a person of ardent zeal; as, an *enthusiast* in poetry or music. 3. One of elevated fancy or exalted ideals. *Dryden*" (WD 400). For English Romantic poets, fancy and enthusiasm are more ambiguous terms, even if fancy is frequently feminized. In chapter 4 of the *Biographia Literaria*, Coleridge says that imagination and fancy are different faculties. Fancy is the lower aggregating and associative power of the mind. Nevertheless, for him, fancy and imagination are necessary. Shakespeare

> possessed fancy; fancy [is] considered as the faculty of bringing together images dissimilar in the main by some one point or more of likeness distinguished: *e.g.*, Full gently now she takes him by the hand, / A lily prison'd in a gaol of snow, / Or ivory in an alabaster band: / So white a friend engirts so white a foe. Still mounting, we find undoubted proof in his mind of imagination, or the power by which one image or feeling is made to modify many others, and by a sort of *fusion to force many into one*;—that which afterwards showed itself in such might and energy in *Lear*, where the deep anguish of a father spreads the feeling of ingratitude and cruelty over the very elements of heaven. (CWS 56–57)

Walter Birch, in "A Sermon on the Prevalence of Infidelity and Enthusiasm" preached in the parish church of St. Peter, Colchester, on Tuesday, July 28, 1818, at the visitation of the Lord Bishop of Lindon, Oxford 1818, defined *enthusiasm* as "the offspring of presumption; of a presumption, the highest and most perilous *in kind* that it is possible to conceive; for it is essential to *her* [my italics] nature to assume the fact, upon inadequate grounds, of an extraordinary communication of notions, figures, powers, or authority, from above. Instead of submitting *her* opinion on this point, or indeed on any other, to the rule of Scripture." (C 494). Coleridge objected to the mixture of appropriate and inappropriate terms used by the minister: "I am convinced," he wrote in the margin,

> that the disease of the age is want of enthusiasm, and a tending to fanaticism. . . . Enthusiasm is the absorption of the individual in the object contemplated from the vividness and or intensity of his conceptions and convictions: fanaticism is heat. . . . The enthusiast, on the contrary, is a solitary, who lives in a world of his own peopling and for that cause is disinclined to outward action. . . . I am fully aware that the words [*enthusiasm* and *fanaticism*] are used by the best writers indifferently, but such must be the case in very many words in a composite language such as the English, before they are desynonymized. Thus imagination and fancy; chronical and temporal, and many other. (C 495–97)

The copy of Birch's sermon containing Coleridge's annotations is missing. The Princeton edition has taken them from *Literary Remains II*, Lost List, edited by his daughter and son-in-law in 1836–39.

"Fancy" is an irredeemably feminine word for most Americans. In our democratic culture men are not encouraged to display elevated fancy or exalted ideals. Webster says it is contracted from *fantasy*. Fancy: false notion, caprice, whim. Fancy, *v.i.* "If our search has reached no farther than simile and metaphor, we rather *fancy* than know. *Locke*" (WD 437). Walt Whitman's "Good-bye my Fancy! / Farewell dear mate, dear love! / . . . . Good-bye—and hail! my Fancy" (LG 458–59) is a truant exception in canonical American literary expression. In *Pierre, or The Ambiguities*, Herman Melville's doomed hero is an enthusiast. Bartleby's "I would prefer not to" is an antinomian gesture. " 'I prefer not to,' he respectfully and slowly said, and mildly disappeared" (PT 45).

* * *

The Birth-mark

"It is one thing for me to come before a public magistracy and there to speak what they would have me to speak and another when a man comes to me in a way of friendship privately there is difference in that": Mrs. Hutchinson to Governor Winthrop at her examination by the Court at Newtowne, 1637 (AC 319). "What if the matter be all one," the Governor answered.

F. O. Matthiessen increasingly banished his homosexuality from his public and intellectual life as a professor and critic. The Preface to *American Renaissance* ends with the name of a place—Kittery, Maine—and a date, April 1941. He often lived there with the painter Russell Cheney. The two were lovers and companions for over twenty years, until Cheney's death in 1945. When they were away from each other, and they often were because of separate careers, they wrote daily letters. Matthiessen later willed the 3,100 letters to a Yale classmate with an allegorical or symbolic name: Hyde. Apparently, Matthiessen thought of this private correspondence as "journal-letters" or a "continued journal." Louis Hyde subsequently edited a selection of the correspondence-journal called *Rat & the Devil: Journal Letters of F. O. Matthiessen and Russell Cheney.* Matthiessen's other letters, the public, respectable ones, are in the Beinecke Rare Book and Manuscript Library at Yale. In his Introduction to the suggestively titled *Rat & the Devil,* (nicknames the two men used with each other), Hyde assures readers that there is nothing "mean, narrow, selfish, ingrown, sensual" in this record of an "all-encompassing bond between two men" (RD 12). The editor also cites an entry on Matthiessen in the *Dictionary of American Biography.* "For most of his students and younger colleagues Matthiessen's homosexuality was suggested, if at all, only by the fact that his circle was more predominantly heterosexual than was usual in Harvard literary groups of the time and that he was unusually hostile to homosexual colleagues who mixed their academic and social relations" (RD 12).

"Dearest Rat . . . 'The splendid untrammeled freedom of love'—that's the essence of it all, right. . . . Our union has no name, no label; in the world it does not exist. It is simply the unpalpable, inexpressible fullness of our lives" (RD 46).

In 1924, when F. O. Matthiessen wrote this letter to Russell Cheney, he had recently graduated from Yale and was studying at Oxford as a Rhodes Scholar. The early letters show how deeply the youthful Matthiessen was inspired by Shelley's youthful idealism, his political and sexual radicalism. A letter to Cheney written February 5, 1925, discusses the poet's expulsion from Eton because he and James Hogg had written an essay called "The Necessity of Atheism." The letter ends: "Thank God I didnt go directly from Yale to an American graduate school, and bury myself in the mechanical grind. Here [Oxford] I have been able to pick and choose, and will know definitely what I want when I put my back to the Harvard mill for grinding out PhDs. And at last will come the time when I can express to classes and perhaps in books some of the million things that I have been taking in" (RD 79).

Jonathan Arac, in "F. O. Matthiessen: Authorizing an American Renaissance," points out that T. S. Eliot's insistence on "form" and "impersonality" in poetry increasingly cast a heavy influence on Matthiessen's reading. In 1941 the author of *American Renaissance*, under the influence of Eliot's critical dismissal of Shelley, downplayed his influence on Melville and deplored it in Hawthorne. In the chapter called "Allegory and Symbolism," Matthiessen quoted a passage from an original notebook entry Hawthorne later reworked for the introduction to *Mosses*, about the strange play of reflections in water: "I am half convinced that the reflection [of tree and sky in the Concord River] is indeed the reality—the real thing which Nature imperfectly images to our grosser sense. At all events, the disembodied shadow is nearest to the soul." Matthiessen here added: "That passage is full of Neo-Platonic pitfalls for the artist. It recalls Shelley's similar preference for scenery imaged in water, because it was one remove further from what was actually seen and grasped; and the unfortunate results are apparent in the thinness of the texture of his lines when contrasted with the richer tactual imagery of Keats. Far worse, Hawthorne's terms seem here to converge with those of Sophia, who, when her body had been sluggish about leaving the house on a fine day, announced that 'Ideality led me out'" (AR 259).

"Deezie, [Devil] on the back of your letter this morning was a shopping list, and with a flood the actual scene of your life—your being alive there—was all through me. It sort of took my breath it was so real—as though I'd reached out and touched you. . . ."

sugar
cocoa
cereal
eggs
bread
salt
pepper

Oct 7, 1929 (RD 158)

In 1925, F. O. Matthiessen excitedly wrote to Russell Cheney: "Shelley's letters take me more and more into his nature." An author takes the reader in. Enchantment of the other. When he was writing *American Renaissance*, Matthiessen was particularly interested in Melville's marginalia. Marks in the margin are immediate reflections. Reflection is also a coupling. Marginal notes are not works. "The Crimson Hand expressed the ineludible gripe in which mortality clutches the highest and purest of earthly mould, degrading them into kindred with the lowest, and even with the very brutes, like whom their invisible frames return to dust" (H 766). Melville underlined the two words in his copy of *Mosses* and drew a line in the right-hand margin. We are always returning to unconscious talking. *Gripe*: to seize, to hold fast, to clutch, pinch, to feel the colic. Erogenous zones are ineludibly linked to the unconscious. The devil in manuscript. Repression says to write notes on it. " 'Then sir,' said the stranger, who proved a lawyer, 'you are responsible for the man you left there. He refuses to do any copying; he refuses to do anything; he says he prefers not to; and he refuses to quit the premises' " (PT 39). Un-useful scholarship. Are substitutes couples? Marginalia may be called speed reading or ghost writing.

"*Right* originally means *straight; wrong* means *twisted . . . transgression*, the crossing of a *line*" (EN 33). Trespassing. Just what I was thinking. That's why daughters are dumb. Presence is necessary. Bartleby *mildly* disappears.

Elizabeth Hawthorne loved walking and reading. Nathaniel Hawthorne warned his wife, Sophia, not to walk with his sister "because she is indefatigable, and also wants to walk half round the world, when once she is out-of-doors" (EH 316). Elizabeth's written recollections of her brother are in the form of letters written to James T. Fields. He asked for them when he was writing Hawthorne's biography. Then he didn't use them.

In 1941, for the chapter on Melville called "Reassertion of the Heart," the author of *The Achievement of T. S. Eliot* and *American Renaissance* cited Melville's marking in Arnold's *Empedocles on Etna* "The brave impetuous heart yields everywhere / To the subtle contriving head" (AR 488). Bartleby may have once been a subordinate clerk in the Dead Letter Office at Washington. He would have continually handled undelivered letters. He would have gathered them together to be burned.

The long chapter on Whitman in *American Renaissance: Art and Ex-*

pression in the Age of Emerson and Whitman is utterly conflicted. Matthiessen's Preface to *American Renaissance* assures readers that he wishes "to pass beyond such interrelations to basic formulations about the nature of literature" (AR xiii). "Ah Bartleby! Ah humanity!" (PT 45) What is the nature of epistolary enthusiasm?

In 1924, "Devil" (Matthiessen), then a young graduate student, wrote to Cheney ("Rat"):

> Eton with its late perpendicular chapel modelled after King's College, Cambridge. Eton with its red-brick courts. Eton where Shelley was miserable, and where he left his name carved on the oak wainscoting along with Walpole's and Pitt's and some ten thousand others.
>
> I carried Walt Whitman in my pocket. Thats another thing you've started me doing, reading Whitman. Not solely because it gives me an intellectual kick the way it did last year, but because I'm living it. How about this to characterize our relationship?
>
> > I announce the great individual, fluid as nature, chaste,
> > affectionate, compassionate, fully-armed.
> > I announce a life that shall be copious, vehement, spiritual, bold,
> > And I announce an old age that shall lightly and joyfully meet
> > its translation.
>
> Those rich, embracing adjectives may not sum it all up, but they certainly include a great many of the elements. (RD 26)

In England, in 1924, Walt Whitman inspired a young American idealist to accept his sexuality in bold and romantic terms.

In New England, seventeen years later, Matthiessen's book about "mid-nineteenth century *re-birth*" begins with a bracing epigraph from Emerson's essay "Representative Men." The long final chapter on Whitman falters over the creative intentions of the author of *Leaves of Grass*. Commenting on the opening of "Song of Myself," the utterly conflicted cultural historian and critic wrote:

> Readers with a distaste for loosely defined mysticism have plenty of grounds for objection in the way the poet's belief in divine inspiration is clothed in imagery that obscures all distinctions between body and soul by portraying the soul as merely the sexual agent. Moreover, in the passivity of the poet's body there is a quality vaguely pathological and homosexual. This is in keeping with the regressive, infantile fluidity, imaginatively polyperverse, which breaks down all mature

> barriers, a little further on in 'Song of Myself,' to declare that he is 'maternal as well as paternal, a child as well as a man' (AR 535).

The public, critical Matthiessen divorced himself from the immediacy of Whitman the maternal enthusiast. Scholarship should be applied for good, not for pampering. Love in an earlier beginning is here consigned to the immature margins: feminized—with mothers. Matthiessen's rebukes and defenses of Whitman may be the expression of a war in himself between a covenant of faith and a covenant of works. We will not read it here. "It is blank here, for reasons" (LG 356). An ocean of inaudible expression. An American educator. A careful citizen. A mind so terribly aware.

These 3,100 journal-letters, these 1,600,000 untrammeled marks of presentation: "It is dark here underground, it is not evil or pain here, it is blank here, for reasons. / . . . I turn but do not extricate myself. / Confused, a past-reading, another, but with darkness yet" (LG 355–56).

Oh hunger that crosses the bridge between

Jonathan Arac points out that the American Civil War isn't even indexed in F. O. Matthiessen's book about mid-nineteenth-century rebirth.

I have neglected to mention Matthiessen's many and varied leftist political affiliations during the 1930s and 1940s. Maybe my reading domesticates him.

F. O. Matthiessen ended the final section of the "Allegory and Symbolism" chapter, called "Coda," by citing D. H. Lawrence: "An allegorical image has a *meaning*. Mr. Facing-both-ways has a meaning. But I defy you to lay your finger on the full meaning of Janus, who is a symbol" (AR 315).

When Matthiessen jumped from a window of the Manger Hotel during the night of March 31, 1950, he left behind the keys to his apartment on Beacon Hill and a note: "I have taken this room in order to do what I have to do . . . Please notify Harvard University—where I have been a professor. I am exhausted . . . I can no longer believe that I can continue to be of use to my profession and my friends. I hope that my friends will be able to believe that I still love them in spite of this desperate act." On the back of the page he wrote: "I should like to be buried beside my mother in the cemetery at Springfield, Mass. My sister . . . will know about this. Please notify, *but not until morning* . . . Mrs. Farwell Knapp . . . or Mrs. Ruth Putnam. I would like them to go to my apartment and to see that the letters on the desk are mailed" (RD 367).

In 1941 women were banished from Matthiessen's *American Renaissance: Art and Expression in the Age of Emerson and Whitman.* At one time he intended to include Margart Fuller but thought better of it. Matthiessen ended his section called "Acknowledgements" this way: "The true function of scholarship as of society is not to stake out claims on which others must not trespass, but to provide a community of knowledge in which others may share" (AR xx).

* * *

So we must meet apart –
You there – I . here –
With just the door ajar
That Oceans are . and Prayer –
And that White Sustenance –
Despair . + Exercise - privilege -

(MBED 2:797)

During the 1950s, although I was only a high school student, I was already a library cormorant. I needed out-of-the-way volumes from Widener Library. My father said it would be trespassing if I went into the stacks to find them. I could come with him only as far as the second-floor entrance. There I waited while he entered the guarded territory to hunt for books. At the margin of the stacks of Widener there are three small dioramas built into the wall. Conceived in 1936, these simulations were meant to celebrate the tricentennial of Harvard College. Each one holds a bird's-eye view of Cambridge then and before. These minature versions of a past that wasn't and a present that isn't are locked in place behind glass in the entrance hall to Widener Library.

Hawthorne's sister first read Shakespeare's *As You Like It* when she was nine. The play made her wish for an outdoor life. "It has always seemed to me," Elizabeth wrote to Una, her niece, "that there must be agreeable people in the woods like those in the Forest of Arden" (EH 316). Thoreau said, in an essay called "Walking," that in literature it is only the wild that attracts us. What is forbidden is wild. The stacks of Widener Library and of all great libraries in the world are still the wild to me. Thoreau went to the woods because he wished to live deliberately in order to give a true account in his next excursion. I go to libraries because they are the ocean.

* * *

and so she sate
Looking upon the waves; on the bare strand
Upon the sea-mark a small boat did wait.
("Revolt of Islam," s 44)

During the 1980s and 1990s a group of scholars, with Donald H. Rieman acting as the General Editor, has been working on the Bodleian Shelley Manuscripts. Each volume, published by the Garland Press, is a facsimile edition with full transcription and scholarly apparatus. Rieman says, in the Foreword to volume 7: "The chief aim of the Bodleian Shelley Manuscripts is neither textual nor critical, but archival. That is, our collective primary task is to make available to readers around the world—both in quality photofacsimiles and in introductions, bibliographical descriptions, and textual notes that clarify the representations in those facsimiles—the materials in the literary manuscripts of Percy Bysshe Shelley and Mary W. Shelley in the Bodleian Library, Oxford" (B 7:vii). The result is not an explication of Shelley's poetics; rather it represents a group of scholars from various disciplines who are working together with a variety of methodologies to solve problems and to raise new questions for readers of Shelley. In Germany another group of co-editors and scholars is working on a new critical edition of Hölderlin's late drafts and fragments. Richard Sieburth writes in the introduction to his translation of Friedrich Hölderlin's *Hymns and Fragments*: "[The editors of the Frankfurt Hölderlin] by presenting Hölderlin's texts as events rather than objects, as processes rather than products, [convert] the reader from passive consumer into active participant in the genesis of the poem, while at the same time calling attention to the fundamentally historical character of both the reader's and writer's activity" (HF 35).

Dickinson is a poet of the order of Shelley and Hölderlin. She is one of the greatest poets who ever wrote in English. The trace of her unapprehended passage through letters disturbs the order of a world where commerce is reality and authoritative editions freeze poems into artifacts. Why isn't there a similar editorial project working now to show the layerings and fragile immediacies of her multifacted visual and verbal productions? Why is there still no substantial critique of the history of these authorized and unauthorized texts? Foucault's questions in "What Is an Author?": "What are the modes of existence of this discourse? Where does it come from; how is it circulated; who controls it?" are relevant here. New questions have been heard and new placements determined for poets who are men. How can "the subject (and its substitutes) . . . be stripped of its creative role and analyzed as a complex and variable function of discourse" (LCP 138) before we have been allowed to even see what *she, Emily Dickinson*, reveals of her most profound self in the multiple multilayered scripts, sets, notes, and scraps she left us? I cannot murmur indifferently: "What matter who's speaking?" I emphatically insist it does matter who's speaking. The presentation of the author's, Emily Dickinson's, texts through the cooperative editing of a facsimile edition of all of the poems, letters, and fragments owned by the Houghton Library at Harvard University, the Amherst College Library, and the Boston Public Library, with full transcription and scholarly apparatus, by a group of scholars working together is long overdue.

* * *

When Shelley sailed from Leghorn on July 8, 1822, he had recently been reworking his unfinished drama, *Charles I*. For the voyage home to San Terenzo he took along three memorandum books. After the sunken *Don Juan*—which the poet had hoped to rechristen *Ariel*—was raised, Captain Daniel Roberts pulled them from the wreck.

One of these rough-draft notebooks includes the holograph fair copy of over a quarter of "A Defence of Poetry," and drafts for the Preface and some stanzas from "Adonais." This notebook, pulled from the bottom of the sea, has now been designated "Bodleian Manuscript Shelley adds. e. 20." It is heavily damaged by water, mildew, and restoration. The poet wrote in this early manuscript a draft of the essay "A Defence."

A P oet is a~~s~~- nightin gale who sits

< > dar kness & sings to cheer its own

so li tude w ith s w eet sounds; his

au ditors are as m en entr anced by

an unseen
the me lody of ~~the~~ ~~in-vis-i-ble~~ mus ician

who
& feel that they are m ov ed &

s oftened, yet know not, w hence or w hy.

(B 169)

In the margin of his copy of *Shelley Memorials: From Authentic Sources . . . To Which Is Added a Letter on Christianity, by Percy Bysshe Shelley*, edited by Lady Jane Gibson Shelley and published by Ticknor Fields, Boston, 1859, Herman Melville underlined and checked this passage from a letter written by the poet to Mrs. Gisborne, May 8, 1820: "Take care of yourselves, and do *you* not forget your nightly journal. *The silent dews renew the grass without effort in the night.* I mean to write to you, but not to-day" (MM 2:505).

Anne Hutchinson is the rose at the threshold of *The Birth-mark: unsettling the wilderness in American literary history*. In this dark allegory—the world—wild roses are veils before trespass.

* * *

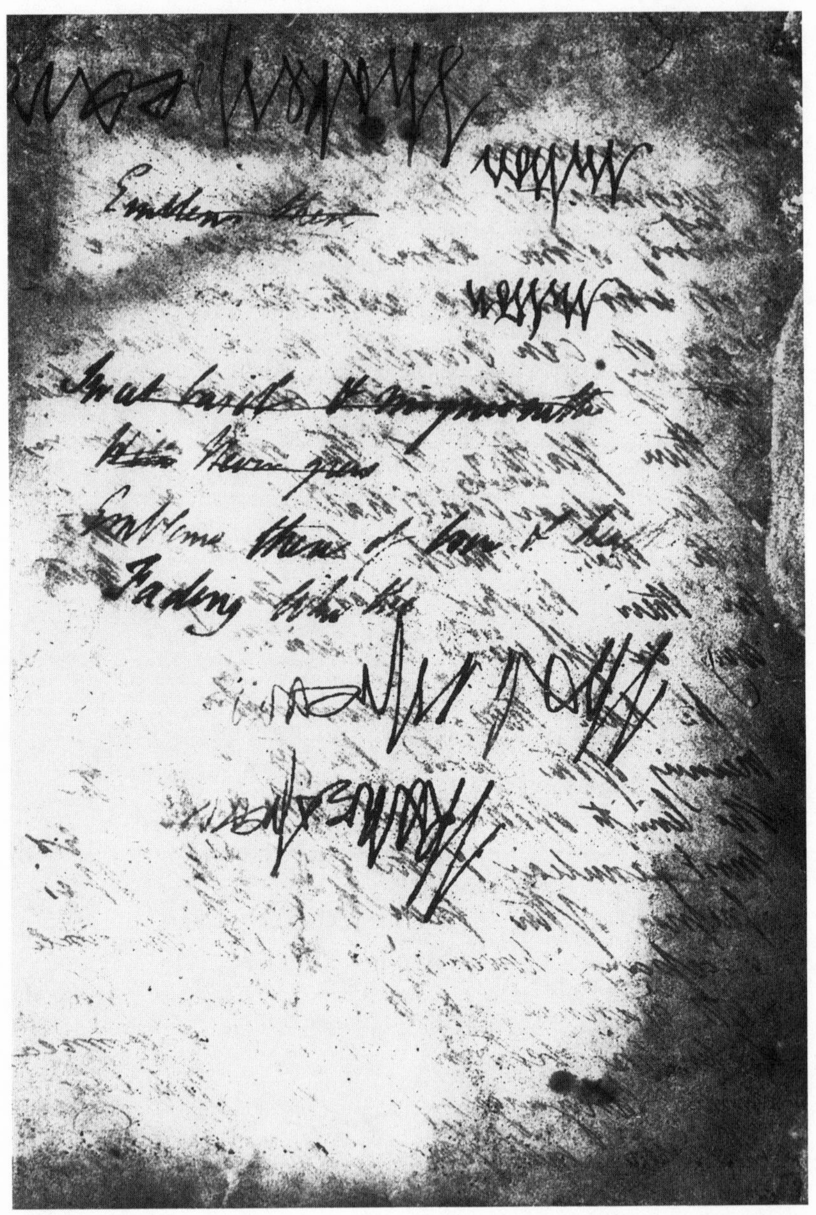

Page from Shelley's Manuscript Book (Bodleian MS. Shelley adds. e. 20: Quire II Folio 2 Recto = 2 Recto). Transcription (right) by Donald H. Reiman and Hélène Dworzan Reiman in *The Bodleian Shelley Manuscripts: A Facsimile Edition, with Full Transcriptions and Scholarly Apparatus*, Volume VII, (New York, 1989), 138–39. Used by permission of the Bodleian Library, University of Oxford.

2

A

Shakespeare

Milton

~~Emblem---[?these]-~~

Milton

Sweet~~--basil---&--mignionette~~

~~Wi[th]~~ ~~Never--grew~~

Emblems these of love & health

F a ding like the

Shakespe[ ]

Shakespe[ ]

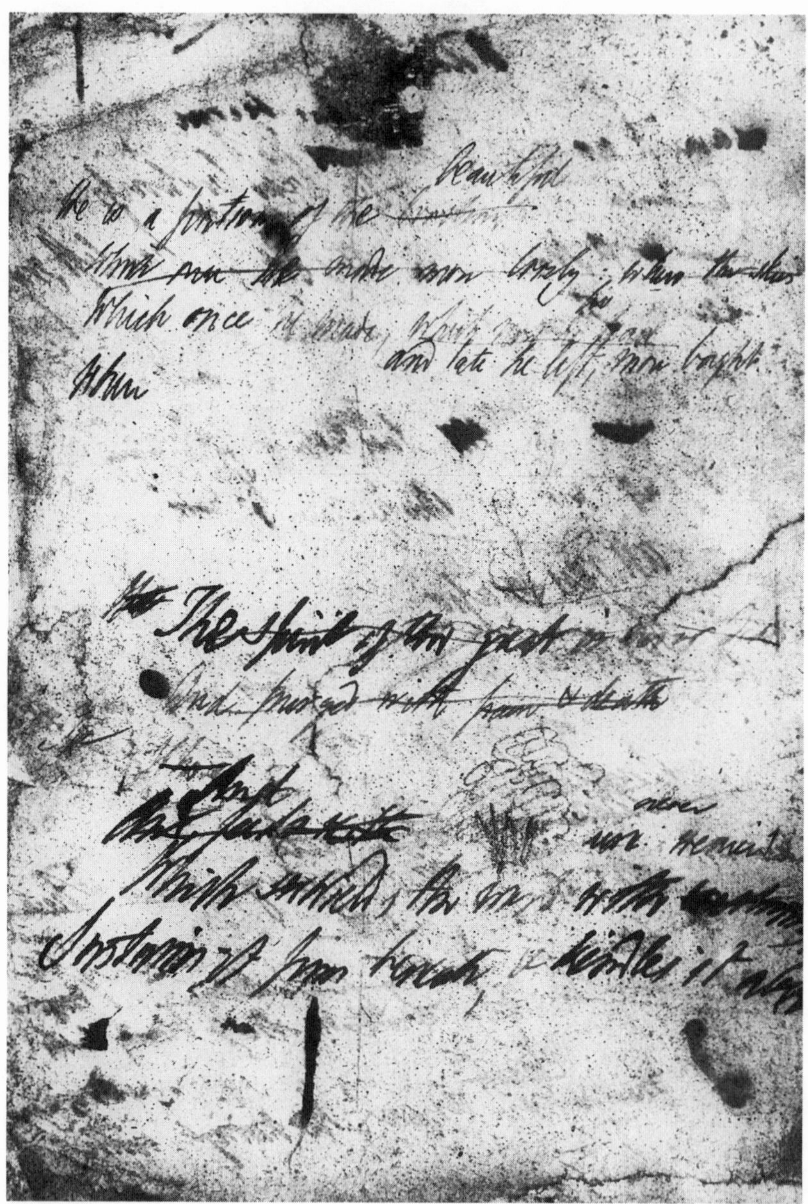

Page from Shelley's Manuscript Book (Bodleian MS. Shelley adds. e. 20: Quire VI Folio 4 Verso = 37 verso. Transcription (right) by Donald H. Reiman and Hélène Dworzan Reiman in *The Bodleian Shelley Manuscripts: A Facsimile Edition, with Full Transcriptions and Scholarly Apparatus*, Volume VII, (New York, 1989), 292–93. Used by permission of the Bodleian Library, University of Oxford.

beautiful
He is a portion of the ~~-loveliness~~

Which ~~-once--he--made--more--lovely-+--where--the--skies~~

4 Which once he made, ~~which--now--he-[?leave<>-]~~
and late he left, more bright

Where

[SKETCH
OF
TREES]

[He]
The~~--spirit--of--the--great--is--never--dead~~

~~And--purged--with--pain--&--death~~

[SKETCH
OF
TREES]

10 ~~The Who-~~
~~And~~
~~And--feels--with~~
never
[un] wearied
Which [~~eer~~] wields the world with [?~~eer~~]~~sustainting~~
love

15 Sustains it from beneath, & kindles it above

Submarginalia

SAMUEL TAYLOR COLERIDGE: I am, & ever have been, a great reader—& have read almost every thing—a library-cormorant—I am *deep* in all out of the way books, whether of the monkish times, or of the puritanical aera—I have read & digested most of the Historical Writers—; but I do not *like* History. Metaphysics, & Poetry, & "Facts of Mind"—(i.e. Accounts of all the strange phantasms that ever possessed your philosophy-dreamers from Tauth, the Egyptian to Taylor, the English Pagan,) are my darling Studies.—In short, I seldom read except to amuse myself—& I am almost always reading (C ciii)

The cormorant is a glossy, black water bird often called sea-raven. Cormorants are widely dispersed over the Northern Hemisphere and both sides of the Atlantic Ocean. They are underwater swimmers who feed on fish; they are voracious. Cormorants dive and swim along the ocean bottom, swiftly scanning every hole or pool, searching for prey. When a fish is sighted, it is seized at once, and the bird rises to the surface with the captive in its beak. Swimming under clear water, they seem to be flying.

These birds, if taken when young from the nest, can be trained to fish for a keeper. In sixteenth- and seventeenth-century England cormorant fishing was a sport. James I particularly enjoyed it. In 1618 he appointed a "master of the royal cormorants," and a house and ponds were built for his cormorants, ospreys, and otters. In *Paradise Lost*, Milton makes the bird a similitude for Satan. "So clomb this first grand Thief into God's fold; / So since into his Chruch lewd hirelings climb. / Thence up he flew, and on the Tree of Life, / The middle tree and highest there that grew, / Sat like a cormorant" (PL Bk. 4:192–96).

Cormorants are strand birds; they occupy cliffs by the ocean, where they perch upright on rocks, often motionless for long periods of time, with wings extended.

* * *

COTTON MATHER: I write the *Wonders* of the CHRISTIAN RELIGION, flying from the Depravations of *Europe*, to the *American Strand*: And, assisted by the Holy Author of that *Religion*, I do, with all Conscience of *Truth*, required therein by Him, who is the *Truth* it self, Report the *Wonderful Displays* of His Infinite Power, Wisdom, Goodness, and Faithfulness, wherewith His Divine Providence hath *Irradiated* an *Indian Wilderness*. (MC 89)

A strand is the part of a shore lying between tidemarks.

A strand is a filament or fiber laid flat to form a unit for twisting or braiding into yarn, thread, rope, or cordage. A strand could be a stalk of grass, a string of pearls, barbs or fibers of feathers, a filament of hair. Molecular changes in the brain are caused by impulses traveling along the strands of nerve fibers.

"God brought Moses law into the world to be as a strand to the inundation of impiety"—Jeremy Taylor, 1649.

Strand, *v.t.*, to drift or be driven on shore.

JOHN WINTHROP (1637): There was an old woman in Ipswich, who came out of England blind and deaf, yet her son could make her understand any thing, and know any man's name by her sense of feeling. He would write upon her hand some letters of the name, and by other such motions would inform her. This the governor himself had || trial of|| ||tried often|| when he was at Ipswich. (WH 1:235)

Motherly Piety: an anonymous old woman of Ipswich, swaddled in silence, stranded in darkness, serves as Governor Winthrop's exemplary version during the disorderly days of the birth of his colony, when Mrs. Hutchinson, a mother and a midwife, impiously dared to preach and prophesy.

Unknownness did your sense of touch re-trace my own nothingness? Finger the way you imagined I am anything. Is your blind gaze sensible? Is my question a solecism? Is a poetics of intervening absence an oxymoron? Do we go anywhere? I will twine feathers, prickings, rulings, wampum beads, chance echoes, sprays of lace in the place of your name. No more apprehension this side of history. Look we are reading a false conception.

Folklore of the cormorant: In China there is a superstition that the bird isn't born from eggs. "The hare spits its young out, the cormorant spits its fledglings out," goes an old saying. In ancient Japan, holding a cormorant was supposed to bring about an easy delivery; for the same reason a cormorant feather was grasped in the hand of a woman just as she was giving birth (DC 255).

* * *

Negative Transference

In 1977, Kenneth Murdock's Introduction to the Harvard Belknap Edition of Cotton Mather's *Magnalia Christi Americana: or, The Ecclesiastical History of New-England, from Its First Planting in the Year 1620, unto the Year of Our* LORD, *1698, in Seven* BOOKS, cites his friend and colleague Perry Miller: "The intellectual history of New England up to 1720 can be written as though the [witchcraft] persecution in Massachusetts had never taken place. It had no effect on the ecclesiastical or political situation, it does not figure in the institutional or ideological development" of New England (MC 9).

Mather would not have agreed in 1700, the year he finished writing "the Church History of this countrey" (MC 25). The antinomian controversy, the witchcraft trials, cases of possession, and captivity narratives are all included in *Magnalia* and in other books, sermons, and pamphlets he wrote. Although women have troublesome, baffling, potentially transgressive natures, at least they exist. In 1941, Emily Dickinson is a blank in F. O. Matthiessen's *American Renaissance: Art and Expression in the Age of Emerson and Whitman.*

Some of Emily Dickinson's surviving manuscripts and letters have been cut apart with scissors. Sometimes pages have been torn to shreds, leaving a single or double strand of words on the brink of the central blank. In the 1958 edition of *The Letters of Emily Dickinson*, her editor, Thomas H. Johnson, pieced torn unities together. Sometimes he lengthened and recombined strands of "unrelated thoughts" or "fragment scraps" and placed them in a category called "Prose Fragments," as if these threaded filaments of letters were too disorderly to qualify as poetry.

Strand, *noun*, from the Saxon *strand*, is the shore or beach of the sea, of the ocean or of a large lake or navigable river. A margin is a border, edge, brink, or verge of land. In botany a margin is the edge of a leaf. In books the margin is the edge of a page, left blank or to be filled in with notes.

Possibly in late 1885, Emily Dickinson wrote in a letter to her sister-in-law Susan:

Emerging from an Abyss, and reentering it—that is Life, is it not, Dear?

The tie between us is very fine, but a Hair never dissolves (L 1024)

1861]

Death sets a Thing significant
The Eye had hurried by
Except a perished Creature
Entreat us tenderly

To ponder little Workmanships
In Crayon , or in Wool ,
With " This was last Her
fingers did " -
Industrius until -

The Thimble weighed too heavy -
The stitches stopped - themselves.
And then 'twas put among
the Dust
Upon the Closet shelves -

A Book I have -a friend gave -
Whose Pencil - here and there -
Had notched the place that
pleased Him -
At Rest - His fingers are -

Now - when I read - I read
not -
For interrupting Tears -
Obliterate the Etchings
Too Costly for Repairs .

(MBED 2:745–46)

Maybe margins shelter the inapprehensible Imaginary of poetry.

* * *

lo tsi k'o am, to have a ring around one's neck like a cormorant, i.e., not to be wholly one's own master.

In China and Japan cormorants are domesticated. A ring or strap around the bird's neck is a symbol of its bondage. An owner needs some way to bridle and direct his worker-pet's fishing, so a cord or strap of hemp is strung around the bird's neck, then attached to a leash or line. Neck rings made from straw, rattan, bamboo, or iron serve the same purpose as the horse's bit, the water buffalo's nose ring, the falcon's leash and hood; the noose also prevents the bird from swallowing large fish.

"[I]n the last and highest stage of development," writes Berthold Laufer in *The Domestication of the Cormorant in China and Japan*, "the neck-collar is simply discarded. . . . At this stage of the game the birds are disciplined to such a degree of perfection that they fish in unrestrained and absolute freedom. A well trained cormorant, while on duty, will not swallow any fish whether large or small; he knows his business and his lord" (DC 242).

* * *

An Idea of Wilderness

Magnalia is intended to be a historical account of the settlement and religious history of New England. Although Mather called his *Magnalia* a "History," its seven volumes could be called "Marginalia" *Christi Americana*. The general style is oddly fixed and declamatory; yet the provincial nonconformist author constantly disrupts the forward trajectory of his written "service . . . for the Church of God, not only here but abroad in Europe," with blizzards of anecdotes, anagrams, prefatory poems, dedications, epigrams, memories, lists of ministers and magistrates, puns, paradoxes, "antiquities," remarks, laments, furious opinions, recollections, exaggerations, fabrications, "Examples," wonders, spontaneous other versions. Short laudatory biographical sketches of the lives of "stars of the first magnitudes in our heavens" are constructed from miscellaneous documentation and distant recollection and punctuated with sudden self-revealing reverse opinion. Kenneth Murdock gave up after editing Books 1 and 2.* He says that Mather the reader "was primarily a smatterer, constantly skimming through whole volumes in search of passages containing ideas which he thought he could develop in his own way or which might serve him as appropriate quotations for use in his own writing" (MC 23). *Magnalia* was far too lengthy a document to be published in Massachusetts. On June 4, 1700, Mather wrote in his Diary: "I this Day putt up my *Church-History*,

*Whenever possible in these essays I use Murdock's edition of *Magnalia*. Much of the Hutchinson controversy and the life of John Cotton occurs in later books, so it was necessary to use the Andrus 1855 edition.

and pen down Directions about the publishing it. It is a work of near 300 sheets; and has lain by me, diverse years, for want of a fitt opportunity to send it. A Gentleman, just now sailing for *England*, undertakes the care of it; and by his Hand I send it for *London*" (MC 27). When Mather received the textual production of his voluminous work back from the "depravations of Europe" two years later, he was horrified by the numerous printer's errors.

In 1818, William Tudor, the first editor of the *North American Review*, published a critical essay on the *Magnalia*. According to Murdock, Tudor's attitude represents nineteenth-century opinion of the book. "In this effeminate period . . . a fair perusal of Mather's *Magnalia* is an achievement not to be slighted . . . 800 folio pages in close double columns, even of the most desirable matter, might well cause hesitation. What then must be the effect of a chaotick mass of history, biography, obsolete creeds, witchcraft, and Indian wars, interspersed with bad puns, and numerous quotations in Latin, Greek and Hebrew which rise up like so many decayed, hideous stumps to arrest the eye and deform the surface?" (MC 33). In spite of this judgment it is impossible to imagine Hawthorne's early tales and sketches without the *Magnalia*. The idiosyncratic combination of history, fiction, Scripture, and Elizabethan and baroque drama in *Moby-Dick* recalls Mather's monumental meditative document. Mather was attracted to Camden's idea that letters in a word or name could be rearranged to cabalistically reveal God's hidden purpose. *Magnalia*'s nearly obsessive use of anagram and paradox reflects this belief and can be directly related to verbal compression in Webster's *American Dictionary of the English Language*, Emerson's essays, and Dickinson's poetry and letters: library cormorants all.

The same year William Tudor wrote his derogatory essay in America, Coleridge was preparing his last course of lectures in London. On March 10, 1818, the poet made a notebook entry meant to describe himself. In 1836 his editor daughter and son-in-law placed it after the Preface to the first two volumes of *Literary Remains*.

> ⟨S. T. C.=⟩ who with long and large arm still collected precious Armfuls in whatever direction he pressed forward, yet still took up so much more than he could keep together that those who followed him gleaned more from his continual droppings than he himself brought home—Nay, made stately Corn-ricks therewith, while the Reaper himself was still seen only with a strutting Armful of newly cut Sheaves.—But I should misinform you grossly, if I left you to

> infer that his Collections were a heap of incoherent Miscellanea—No!—the very Contrary—Their variety conjoined with the too great Coherency, the too great both desire & power of referring them in systematic, nay, genetic subordination was that which rendered his schemes gigantic & impracticable, as an Author—& his Conversation less instructive, as a man/—Inopem sua *Copia* fecit, too much was given, all so weighty & brilliant as to preclude choice, & too many to be all received—so that it passed over the Hearers mind like a roar of waters—. (C CXXV)

Coleridge's dissection of his turbulent, sometimes unfathomable literary expression could be a description of *Magnalia Christi Americana*. Even if he had to subsist on provincial libraries, Mather's voracious reading a century earlier rivaled Coleridge's. A provincial library cormorant, utterly in love with words, Mather sometimes resembles Baudelaire's Poet-Albatross. "Le Poète est semblable au prince des nuées / Qui hante la tempête et se rit de l'archer; / Exilé sur le sol au milieu des huées, / Ses ailes de géant l'empêchent de marcher" (FM 32).

* * *

Years before John Livingston Lowes wrote *The Road to Xanadu*, Thomas Wolfe was his student at Harvard. Marginal note 85a to Martin Gardner's edition of *The Annotated Ancient Mariner* tells us "Lowes' belief that Coleridge's creative genius had fed unconsciouly on memories acquired by prodigious reading had much to do with Wolfe's insane attempt, as a student, to read all the books in the Harvard library" (AM 70).

In 1927, when he was working on *Look Homeward, Angel*, Wolfe told a former teacher: "I think I shall call it 'Alone, Alone,' for the idea that broods over it, and in it, and behind it is that we are all strangers upon this earth we walk on—that naked and alone do we come into life, and alone, a stranger, each to each, we live upon it. The title, as you know, I have taken from the poem I love best, 'The Rime of the Ancient Mariner' " (AM 70).

* * *

Coleridge, a cormorant of libraries, dives *deep* in books as if they were a sea. When Thoreau compares readers who devour the sentimental novels in Concord's circulating library to cormorants who will digest anything, he means women (novelists and readers), though he doesn't say the word or use the feminine pronoun. The chapter in *Walden* is called "Reading."

Look Homeward, Angel is a sentimental novel. Walden is only a pond. Ponds can't have strands.

According to the "Editor's Introduction" to *The Collected Works of Samuel Taylor Coleridge* (*Marginalia I: Abbt to Byfield*), Robert Southey, the author of *The Life of Nelson*, allowed Coleridge to write marginal comments in his prized edition of Cotton Mather's *Magnalia Christi Americana*. Southey once recommended Mather's *Ecclesiastical History of New England from Its First Planting* to a friend as "one of the most extraordinary books in the world" (C lxxi, *n*).

Coleridge often penciled notes in the margins of Southey's books; Robert Southey later reverently retraced them in ink for posterity.

* * *

> Yet I was a most fearless child by daylight—ever ready to take the difficult mountain path and outgo my companions' daring in tree-climbing. In those early days we used to spend much of our summer time in trees, greatly to the horror of Mrs. Rickman and some of our London visitors.
>
> On reviewing my earlier childhood, I find the predominant reflection . . . (SD 266)

This is the apprehensive conclusion to Sara Coleridge's brief autobiographical narrative in the form of a letter addressed to her daughter Edith. The autobiography was an epistolary project uncharacteristically never mentioned in her other writings. Edith later published a heavily edited version in *Memoir and Letters of Sara Coleridge* in 1874. Bradford Keyes Mudge in his illuminating study, *Sara Coleridge, A Victorian Daughter: Her Life and Essays*, points out the author's bitter awareness here of her own submarginal status. Sara begins her narrative by precisely noting:

> My father has entered his marriage with my mother and the births of my three brothers with some particularity in a family Bible, given him, as he also notes, by Joseph Cottle on his marriage; the entry of my birth is in my dear mother's hand-writing and this seems like an omen of our life-long separation, for I was never with him for more than a few weeks at a time. He lived not much more, indeed, with his other children, but most of their infancy passed under his eye. Alas! more than any of them I inherited that uneasy health of his, which kept us apart. But I did not mean to start with "alas!" (SD 163)

"The term *marginalia* (singular, *marginale*) refers to anything written by Coleridge in the margins and other blank spaces in the text of a printed book, on flyleaves, end-papers, or the inside or outside of a paperwrapper" (C xxiii). Coleridge's notes on the two front flyleaves in BIBLE *Copy A* can be found in *Marginalia I: Abbt to Byfield*. Five entries were made there in "various hands." They have been consigned by the editors to a section called Annex. Annex is matter printed at the end of a book entry typographically distinct from the marginalia. "Sara Coleridge born December 23, 20 minutes past 6 in the Morning, 1802" (C 413). If Mrs. Coleridge hadn't marked it, the record of Sara's birth would be blank in her family's Holy Bible, containing the Old Testament and the New. All entries in the Annex are in women's hands.

Samuel Taylor Coleridge lavished worry and love on his sons Hartley and Derwent (Berkeley died in infancy) while largely ignoring his daughter Sara until she was old enough to be useful to him. Robert Southey was her uncle. During most of her childhood she and her mother and brothers lived with the Southeys at Greta Hall. A brilliant woman, who could speak six languages, Sara became a poet, translator, opium addict, and library cormorant. When she died in 1852, Henry Reed, a professor of English at the University of Pennsylvania, who had first written to her in 1849 for permission to publish an edition of Coleridge's poetry and became one of her many devoted correspondents, wrote a memoir called "The Daughter of Coleridge." He regretted that she had expended so much of her genius in writing editorial notes, prefaces, and letters: "so varied were her writings and so rich in thought and in the accumulation of knowledge, that they may be compared to the conversation and '*marginalia*' of her father" (HR 22).

In 1829, Sara Coleridge married her cousin, Henry Nelson Coleridge, a lawyer and classical scholar. She was pregnant seven times in thirteen years of marriage; only two children survived. Between her frequent miscarriages Sara suffered several nervous breakdowns. When her father died in 1834, his literary executor, Joseph Henry Green, gave Henry Coleridge the task of collecting, arranging, and editing for publication "the scattered remains of that remarkable mind" (HR 30). Sara collaborated on the immense editorial project; at the same time she was serving as Henry's amanuensis by copying legal documents for him in his poorly paid employment as a barrister-at-law. She and Henry, realizing their interest and the amount of energy the author had expended on other authors, went to a great deal of time, money, and trouble in order to trace, gather, and transcribe Coleridge's marginal notes. In 1843, when Henry died after a long illness, she was left with very little money, a massive and unfinished editorial project, and two young children to educate. Her two brothers also left her all responsibility for the care of her widowed mother. While he was alive, Henry had loaned Hartley and Derwent money; it was never repaid. Somehow Sara, formerly the author of a volume of poetry called *Pretty Lessons in Verse for Small Children*—fairy tales, translations, and various essays, including "On the Disadvantages Resulting from the Possession of Beauty," "Nervousness," "Reply to Strictures of Three Gentlemen upon Carlyle," and "On Mr. Wordsworth's Poem Entitled 'Lines Left on a Yew-tree Seat' "—found time to write a two-hundred-page "Essay on Rationalism," prepare the second edition of her father's *Biographia Literaria* (1847) for publication, edit *Notes and Lectures upon Shakespeare, and Some of the Old Poets and Dramatists, with Other Literary Remains of S. T. Coleridge* (1849), then collect and publish her father's random contributions to newspapers and small magazines in *Essays on His Own Times: Forming a Second Series of the Friend* (1850). In endnote after footnote Sara carefully and precisely defended her father from charges of plagiarism. To refute these charges she dutifully read Schelling, Schlegel, and other German philosophers. "I might as well attempt to run up a river, the water up to my waist as to run through Schelling" (SD 108), she wrote to John Taylor Coleridge. While working on the preparation of *Notes and Lectures*, Sara wrote in her diary:

> No work is so inadequately rewarded either by money or credit as that of editing miscellaneous, fragmentary, immethodical literary remains like those of S. T. C. Such labours cannot be rewarded for they cannot be seen—some of them cannot even be perceived in their effects by the intelligent reader. How many, many mornings, evenings, afternoons have I spent in hunting for some piece of information in order to rectify a statement—to decide whether to retain or withdraw a sentence, or how to turn it—the effect being negative, the silent avoidence of error. . . . But when there is not mere carelessness but a positive coldness in regard to what I have done, I do sometimes feel as if I had been wasting myself a good deal—at least so far as worldly advantage is concerned. (CF 157)

All this time she continued in her effort to collect the volumes from Coleridge's library that had been widely scattered at the time of his death. Until a few days before her death in 1852, at forty-nine, she was still laboring over an edition of her father's poems. When the volume was later published as "edited by Sara and Derwent Coleridge," Derwent gracefully acknowledged his sister had done all of the work.

Shortly before she died, Sara Coleridge recalled her father: "Indeed, he seems ever at my ear, in his books, more especially his marginalia—speaking not personally to me, and yet in a way so natural to my feelings, that *finds* me so fully, and awakens such a strong echo in my mind and heart, that I seem more intimate with him now than ever I was in life" (C lviii). George Whalley, editor of the Princeton *Marginalia*, remarks in his Editor's Introduction, "Harvesting the Marginalia": "Except that Henry and Sara preserved some marginal notes that would now be otherwise lost to us, their work is not very useful to the modern editor" (C cxlvi).

"*What* was I?" Sara asked herself in her autobiographical epistolary "sketch" (SD 265).

* * *

Sir William Hamilton, British diplomat and archaeologist, the husband of Emma Hamilton, Horatio Nelson's mistress, described his philosophy in a letter to the admiral. "My study of antiquities . . . has kept me in constant thought of the perpetual fluctuation of every thing. The whole art is really to live all the *days* of our life; and not with anxious care disturb the sweetest hour that life affords,—which is the present. Admire the Creator, and all his works, to us incomprehensible; and do all the good you can upon earth: and take the chance of eternity without dismay" (MM 2:531). Besides underlining the portions of the passage above in his copy of Southey's *Life of Nelson*, Herman Melville drew three lines in the right margin for emphasis. On the front flyleaf of the book, Elizabeth Shaw Melville wrote: "This book is kept for reference for[m?] 'Billy Budd'—(unfinished)" (MM 2:516).

After Melville's death, Mrs. Melville wrote in her husband's edition of Isaac Disraeli's *The Literary Character*: "My ideas of my husband are so much associated with his books that to part with them would be as it were breaking some of the last ties which still connect me with so beloved an object. The being in the midst of books he has been accustomed to read, and which contain his *marks* and *notes*, will still give him *a sort of existence with me*" (F 194). Harrison Hayford and Merton M. Sealts, Jr., editors of *Billy Budd, Sailor* and *Billy Budd: The Genetic Text*, refer to Mrs. Melville's editorial notations on the original manuscript as marks made by an "alien hand."

* * *

Alienation

lashed in a hammock, hemp around his neck, dragging cables, cordage, without volition under language, in a measure mysteriously woman, Billy drifts fathoms down dreaming *Obey* pinned to a clip now gone. What space to which to extend the arms; at that instant we are all like swimmers. "Fathoms down, fathoms down, how I'll dream fast asleep." Fathom understanding: fathom which wave to think. "O, 'tis me, not the sentence they'll suspend" (BB 132). The ballad is so mutinous without a known author. Fatherless in the same sentence what syllables will flood utterance. Warbling, warbling. Leaving no verb in their eyes

our predestinated depths who fathoms. Strond strund stronde strand. The margin submerges phonic substance. A mother's thread or line is ringed about with silence so poems are

Billy radically alone.

* * *

Bitterness Fire Love Sound Water

To feed these essays I have dived through other people's thoughts with footnotes for compasses and categories for quadrants. I have plagiarized sermons, memorial introductions, epitaphs, anagrams, epigrams, dictionaries here and elsewhere. In the acquisitive spirit I have borrowed back brief earlier brimstone sermons. "What is an author?" asks Michel Foucault in the essay that directly inspired and informed my writing about Anne Hutchinson, Thomas Shepard, John Winthrop, Anne Bradstreet, Mary Rowlandson, James Savage, and Emily Dickinson. Foucault's influence is problematic. This wide-ranging philosopher and library cormorant's eloquent, restless, passionate interrogation of how we have come to be the way we are remains inside the margins of an intellectual enclosure constructed from memories, meditations, delusions, and literary or philosophical speculations of European men. "What is a picture?" Jacques Lacan tells me, at the perceptual level, in its relation to desire, reality appears to be marginal. What are the guises of human sciences when women do speak? In Emmanuel Levinas's terminology: "*A work conceived radically is a movement of the Same towards the Other which never returns to the Same*" (CP 91; italics in original). After 1637, American literary expression couldn't speak English. I am a North American author. I was born in 1937. Into World War II and the rotten sin of man-made mass murder. "I see but you, O warlike pennant! O banner so broad, with stripes, I sing you only" (LG 245). What new path in ethics will lead me away? Love words. Definition is variable. We do not have such a Journal.

My aim in the present study? Ask what form for the form. Print is a phobic response to negligence. Letters should be civil or slang being negligent.

Truth is water. Attraction makes it open.

Bold pencil line in margin across the verso leaf at one extreme why should she write. Their business is to fish. A woman writing with such rebelliousness altogether. Ranging marginalia without a known author I am full of hunger. Print is furious have no page to waste. Yoursebl live on demigorgon offspring fearfnll love. What does a seducer hunt?

Unmediated companion I am what you hunt fettered alone in you.

and we desire. Every flag and twig condemned to market mud in the year before April. A child can be had. Ding-dong. "Little Annie's Ramble." "A LITTLE GIRL, of five years old, in a blue frock and white pantalettes, with brown curling hair and hazel eyes." See pure rhetoric to tell to. But I have gone too far from home. The jury sits in judge. John Bull: "Law is a bottomless pit; it is a cormorant." So it is. Consuming means devour everything. Locke, John, his Treatise on the *Human Understanding*; law-nets are cobwebs. *Clarissa; or the History of a Young Lady*; etymological fancies; more rings I won't pity. Eden. First Part of our unwritten. Cormorant time demanding all. So it was

dear (and ever shall be).

In what language shall I address you? Self-assertion by letter writing. Some Connecticut locality. Factual detail.

Many out-of-the-way volumes, especially books about the Puritan Revolution in England, and books by and about Puritans in seventeenth-century New England are my darling studies, and I used them while I was writing these essays

scattered by the fratricidal Enlightenment

she turns the tables without rejecting Abraham Isaac Jacob. That kind of adoration. The time is autumn morning evening. To collect an error in the shelter of theory send disciples soon.

Every source has another center so is every creator.

A mere slip of the coast at a northern extreme America America all is smooth again. Our lakes of the woods. The double's face I remember all shawled and coming down. It was an emblem of desire. Nothing thwarts desire here. Here are gardens blue backgound wash water. Love is reflected in water. The birds their plumage. Swallows swim so low. Sometimes I dive below the line in such a story September October.

Slips from a particular institution all or one of them.

"Our lady was ful of grace as a stronde ful of watyr." In the idiom deconstruction old women wish to remain in touch. Stranger speak kindly. Sometimes speech divides us. Mixture of midland and northern dialect. Transience. Experience. Wyclif's Bible and Wyclif's sermons. Then once, in Sibbes, His great command as clear a benediction. It was my postmodern editorial decision to turn some sections of the conversion narratives and Mary Dyer's letter into poems. If the name Walden hadn't been taken from an English place, Thoreau thinks he could imagine its original name was *Walled-in* Pond. In *This New Yet Unapproachable America*, Stanley Cavell says the name may come from the Waldensian heresy. "O banner so broad there, with stripes, / flapping up there in the wind," let me enfold tenderness. Even so and by such tracing of far-fetched meandering I hope to stray.

In these essays I have followed the spelling and punctuation of each quoted source. Revisions, deletions, footnotes, spelling, stray marks, and punctuation are usually edited to conform to the requirements of whatever period they are published in. In the flow of time original versions are modernized and again modernized

in the flow of time these copies are copies of copies.

Doubles are counteracted one must draw still. "Come up here soul soul." Two desires. Thrift thrift. Near the surface I'll twine them and put in life. They are not the one. Flapping flapping flapping flapping. Sometimes I know you just from reading.

It is the grace of scholarship. I am indebted to everyone.

Key for "Introduction" and "Submarginalia"

AC	*The Antinomian Controversy*: David Hall, ed.
AM	*The Annotated Ancient Mariner*: Samuel Taylor Coleridge; Martin Gardner, ed.
AR	*American Renaissance: Art and Expression in the Age of Emerson and Whitman*: F. O. Matthiessen.
B	*The Bodleian Shelley Manuscripts*: Donald H. Reiman, ed.
BB	*Billy Budd, Sailor*: Herman Melville; Hayford and Sealts, eds.
C	*The Collected Works of Samuel Taylor Coleridge*, vol. 12, *Marginalia 1*: George Whalley, ed.
CF	*Coleridge Fille*: Earl Leslie Griggs.
CP	*Collected Philosophical Papers*: Emmanuel Levinas.
CWS	*Coleridge's Writings on Shakespeare*: Terence Hawkes, ed.
DC	*The Domestication of the Cormorant in China and Japan*: Berthold Laufer.
EH	"Recollections of Hawthorne by His Sister Elizabeth": Randall Stewart.
EN	*Nature*: Ralph Waldo Emerson.
F	*Byron and Byronism in the Mind and Art of Herman Melville*: Edward Fiess.
FM	*Les Fleurs du mal*: Charles Baudelaire.
H	*Tales and Sketches*: Nathaniel Hawthorne.
HF	*Hymns and Fragments*: Friedrich Hölderlin.
HR	*Sara Coleridge and Henry Reed*: Leslie Nathan Broughton, ed.
L	*The Letters of Emily Dickinson*: Johnson and Ward, eds.
LCP	*Language, Counter-Memory, Practice*: Michel Foucault.
LG	*Leaves of Grass*: Walt Whitman.
MBED	*The Manuscript Books of Emily Dickinson*: R. W. Franklin, ed.
MC	*Magnalia Christi Americana*, Books 1 and 2: Kenneth B. Murdock, ed.
MM	*Melville's Marginalia*: Walker Cowen, ed.
PL	*Paradise Lost*: John Milton.
PS	*Selected Writings of Edgar Allan Poe*.
PT	*The Piazza Tales*. "Bartleby, the Scrivener: A Story of Wall-Street": Herman Melville; Hayford, MacDougall, and Tanselle, eds.
PW	*Complete Works of Edgar Allan Poe*, vol. 16, *Marginalia–Eureka*: James A. Harrison, ed.
RD	*Rat & the Devil; Journal Letters of F. O. Matthiessen and Russell Cheney*: Louis Hyde, ed.
S	*Shelley: Poetical Works*: Thomas Hutchinson, ed.
SD	*Sara Coleridge, A Victorian Daughter: Her Life and Essays*: Bradford Keyes Mudge, ed. and author.
SL	*The Scarlet Letter*: Nathaniel Hawthorne.
TS	*Transport to Summer*: Wallace Stevens.
WD	*An American Dictionary of the English Language*: Noah Webster.
WH	*The History of New England from 1630 to 1649*: John Winthrop; James Savage, ed.

Sources for "Introduction" and "Submarginalia"

Arac, Jonathan. "F. O. Matthiessen: Authorizing an American Renaissance." In *The American Renaissance Reconsidered: Selected Papers from the English Institute, 1982–83*, edited by Walter Benn Michaels and Donald E. Pease. 90–112. Baltimore: The Johns Hopkins University Press, 1985.

Baudelaire, Charles. *Les Fleurs du mal*. Edited by Robert Strick. Paris: Presses Pocket, 1989.

Coleridge, Samuel Taylor. *The Annotated Ancient Mariner*. Edited by Martin Gardner. New York: Bramhall House, 1965.

———. *Coleridge's Writings on Shakespeare*. Edited by Terence Hawkes. New York: Capricorn Books, 1959.

———. *The Collected Works of Samuel Taylor Coleridge*. Vol. 12, *Marginalia I: Abbt to Byfield*. Edited by George Whalley. Princeton, N.J.: Princeton University Press, 1980.

Coleridge, Sara. *Memoir and Letters of Sara Coleridge*. Edited by Edith Coleridge. New York: Harper & Brothers, 1874.

———. *Sara Coleridge and Henry Reed*. Edited by Leslie Nathan Broughton. Ithaca, N.Y.: Cornell University Press, 1937.

Dickinson, Emily. *The Letters of Emily Dickinson*. 3 vols. Edited by Thomas H. Johnson and Theodora Ward. Cambridge, Mass.: The Belknap Press, Harvard University Press, 1958.

———. *The Manuscript Books of Emily Dickinson*. 2 vols. Edited by R. W. Franklin. Cambridge, Mass.: The Belknap Press, Harvard University, 1981.

Emerson, Ralph Waldo. *Nature*. A Facsimile of the First Edition. Boston: Beacon Press, 1989.

Fiess, Edward. *Byron and Byronism in the Mind and Art of Herman Melville*. Ann Arbor, Mich.: University Microfilms, 1965.

Foucault, Michel. *Language, Counter-Memory, Practice: Selected Essays and Interviews*. Edited by Donald F. Bouchard. Ithaca, N.Y.: Cornell University Press, 1977.

Griggs, Earl Leslie. *Coleridge Fille: A Biography of Sara Coleridge*. New York: Oxford University Press, 1940.

Hall, David D. *The Antinomian Controversy, 1636–1638: A Documentary History*. Edited by David D. Hall. Middletown, Conn.: Wesleyan University Press, 1968.

Hawthorne, Nathaniel. *The Scarlet Letter and Other Tales of the Puritans*. Edited by Harry Levin. Boston: Houghton Mifflin, 1961.

———. *Tales and Sketches*. New York: The Library of America, 1982.

Hölderlin, Friedrich. *Hymns and Fragments*. Translated by Richard Sieburth. Princeton, N.J.: Princeton University Press, 1984.

Laufer, Berthold. *The Domestication of the Cormorant in China and Japan*. Field Museum of Natural History Anthropological Series, vol. 18, no. 3. Chicago: Field Museum Press, 1931.

Levinas, Emmanuel. *Collected Philosophical Papers*. Translated by Alphonso Lingis. Boston: Martinus Nijhoff, 1987.

Mather, Cotton. *Magnalia Christi Americana: or, The Ecclesiastical History of New-England*. Hartford, Conn.: Silas Andrus & Son, 1855.

———. *Magnalia Christi Americana*, Books 1 and 2. Edited by Kenneth B. Murdock. Cambridge, Mass.: The Belknap Press, Harvard University Press, 1977.

Matthiessen, F. O. *American Renaissance: Art and Expression in the Age of Emerson and Whitman*. New York: Oxford University Press, 1941.

———. *Rat & the Devil; Journal Letters of F. O. Matthiessen and Russell Cheney*. Edited by Louis Hyde. Hamden, Conn.: Archon Books, 1978.

Melville, Herman. *Billy Budd, Sailor (An Inside Narrative)*. Edited by Harrison Hayford and Merton M. Sealts, Jr. Chicago: University of Chicago Press, 1962.

———. *Melville's Marginalia*. 2 vols. Edited by Walker Cowen. New York: Garland Publishing, 1987.

———. *The Piazza Tales, and Other Prose Pieces*. Edited by Harrison Hayford, Alma A. MacDougall, and G. Thomas Tanselle. Evanston and Chicago: Northwestern University Press and the Newberry Library, 1987.

Milton, John. *The Complete Poetical Works of John Milton*. Edited by Douglas Bush. Boston: Houghton Mifflin, 1965.

Mudge, Bradford Keyes. *Sara Coleridge, A Victorian Daughter: Her Life and Essays*. New Haven, Conn.: Yale University Press, 1989.

Poe, Edgar Allan. *The Complete Works of Edgar Allan Poe*. Vol. 16, *Marginalia–Eureka*. Edited by James A. Harrison. New York: AMS Press, 1965.

———. *Selected Writings of Edgar Allan Poe*. Edited by Edward H. Davidson. Boston: Houghton Mifflin, Riverside Press, 1956.

Shelley, Percy Bysshe. *The Bodleian Shelley Manuscripts: A Facsimile Edition, with Full Transcriptions and Scholarly Apparatus*. Vol. 7. Edited by Donald H. Reiman. New York: Garland Publishing, 1989.

———. *Poetical Works*. Edited by Thomas Hutchinson. New York: Oxford University Press, 1990.

Stevens, Wallace. *Transport to Summer*. New York: Alfred A. Knopf, 1951.

Stewart, Randall. "Recollections of Hawthorne by His Sister Elizabeth." *American Literature* 16 (January 1945): 316–29.

Webster, Noah. *An American Dictionary of the English Language*. Revised and enlarged by Chauncey A. Goodrich. Springfield, Mass.: George and Charles Merriam, 1852.

Whitman, Walt. *Leaves of Grass*. Edited by Emory Holloway. Garden City, N.Y.: Doubleday, 1926.

Winthrop, John. *The History of New England from 1630 to 1649*. 2 vols. Edited by James Savage. Boston: Phelps and Farnham, 1825.

Incloser

MATT.XXV.1–13. "Then shall the kingdom of heaven be likened unto ten virgins, which took their lamps and went forth to meet the bridegroom. And five of them were wise and five were foolish. They that were foolish took their lamps and took no oil with them. But the wise took oil in their vessels with their lamps. While the bridegroom tarried, they all slumbered and slept. And at midnight there was a cry made, Behold the bridegroom cometh: go ye out to meet him. Then all those virgins arose and trimmed their lamps. And the foolish said unto the wise, Give us of your oil, for our lamps are gone out. But the wise answered, saying, Not so, lest there be not enough for us and you; but go ye rather to them that sell, and buy for yourselves. And while they went to buy, the bridegroom came, and they that were ready went in with him to the marriage, and the door was shut. Afterward came also the other virgins, saying, Lord, Lord, open to us. But he answered and said, Verily I say unto you, I know you not. Watch, therefore, for ye know neither the day nor the hour wherein the Son of man cometh." (W 2:13)

—Epigraph to *The Parable of The Ten Virgins Opened and Applied, Being The Substance of Divers Sermons on* MATT. *25:1–3. by Thomas Shepard, published from the Author's own Notes [in 1659], at the Desire of Many, for the Common Benefit of the Lord's People*, "by Jonathan Mitchell, Minister at Cambridge, And Thos. Shepard, Son of the Author, Minister at Charlestown." (Boston: Doctrinal Tract and Book Society, 1852.)

EN-CLŌSE. See INCLOSE.

IN-CLŌSE,′ *v.t.* [Fr. *enclos*; Sp. It. *incluso*; L. *inclusus*, *includo*; *in* and *claudo*, or *cludo*.]

1. To surround; to shut in; to confine on all sides; as, to *inclose* a field with a fence; to *inclose* a fort or an army with troops; to *inclose* a town with walls.

2. To separate from common grounds by a fence; as, to *inclose* lands.

3. To include; to shut or confine; as, to *inclose* trinkets in a box.

4. To environ; to encompass.

5. To cover with a wrapper or envelope; to cover under seal; as, to *inclose* a letter or a bank note.

IN-CLŌS′ER, *n.* He or that which incloses; one who separates land from common grounds by a fence.

—Noah Webster, *An American Dictionary of the English Language*

THOMAS SHEPARD

Anagram: O, a map's thresh'd
(W 3:513)

The first and least of those books [by Shepard] is called, "*The Sincere Convert*:" which the Author would commonly call, *his ragged child*; and once, even after its fourth edition, wrote unto Mr. Giles Firmin thus concerning it: "That which is called, '*The Sincere Convert*:' I have not the book: I once saw it: it was a collection of such notes in a dark town in *England*, which one procuring of me, published them without my will or my privity. I scarce know what it contains, nor do I like to see it; considering the many Σφαλματα *Typographica*, most absurd; and the confession of him that published it, that it comes out much altered from what was first written. (M 1:389)

—Cotton Mather, *Magnalia Christi Americana*

* * *

My writing has been haunted and inspired by a series of texts, woven in shrouds and cordage of classic American nineteenth-century works; they are the buried ones, they body them forth.

The selection of particular examples from a large group is always a social act. By choosing to install certain narratives somewhere between history, mystic speech, and poetry, I have enclosed them in an organization, although I know there are places no classificatory procedure can reach, where connections between words and things we thought existed break off. For me, paradoxes and ironies of fragmentation are particularly compelling.

Every statement is a product of collective desires and divisibilities. Knowledge, no matter how I get it, involves exclusion and repression. National histories hold ruptures and hierarchies. On the scales of global power, what gets crossed over? Foreign accents mark dialogues that delete them. Ambulant vagrant bastardy comes looming through assurance and sanctification.

THOMAS SHEPARD: A long story of conversion, and a hundred to one if some lie or other slip not out with it. Why, the secret meaning is, I pray admire me. (W 2:284)

When we move through the positivism of literary canons and master narratives, we consign ourselves to the legitimation of power, chains of inertia, an apparatus of capture.

BROTHER CRACKBONE HIS WIFE: So I gave up and I was afraid to sing because to sing a lie, Lord teach me and I'll follow thee and heard Lord will break the will of His last work. (C 140)

* * *

A printed book enters social and economic networks of distribution. Does the printing modify an author's intention, or does a text develop itself? Why do certain works go on saying something else? Pierre Macherey says, in *A Theory of Literary Production*, "The work has its beginnings in a break from the usual ways of speaking and writing—a break which sets it apart from all other forms of ideological expression" (TP 52). Roman Jakobson says, in "Dialogue on Time in Language and Literature": "One of the essential differences between spoken and written language can be seen clearly. The former has a purely temporal character, while the latter connects time and space. While the sounds that we hear disappear, when we read we usually have immobile letters before us and the time of the written flow of words is reversible" (V 20). Gertrude Stein says, in "Patriarchal Poetry": "They said they said. / They said they said when they said men. / Men many men many how many many many many men men men said many here" (YS 132). Emily Dickinson writes to her sister-in-law, Susan Gilbert Dickinson: "Moving on in the Dark like Loaded Boats at Night, though there is no Course, there is Boundlessness—" (L 871).

Strange translucencies: letters, phonemes, syllables, rhymes, shorthand segments, alliteration, assonance, meter, form a ladder to an outside state outside of States. Rungs between escape and enclosure are confusing and compelling.

BROTHER CRACKBONE HIS WIFE: And seeing house burned down, I thought it was just and mercy to save life of the child and that I saw not after again my children there. And as my spirit was fiery so to burn all I had, and hence prayed Lord would send fire of word, baptize me with fire. And since the Lord hath set my heart at liberty. (C 140)

* * *

There was the last refuge from search and death; so here (W 2:196).

I am a poet writing near the close of the twentieth century.

Little by little sound grew to be meaning. I cross an invisible line spoken in the first word "Then." Every prescriptive grasp assertion was once a hero reading Samson. There and here I encounter one vagabond formula another pure Idea. To such a land. Yet has haunts. The heart of its falls must be crossed and re-crossed. October strips off cover and quiet conscience.

New England is the place I am. Listening to the clock and the sun whirl dry leaves along. Distinguishing first age from set hour. The eternal and spirit in them.

A poem can prevent onrushing light going out. Narrow path in the teeth of proof. Fire of words will try us. Grace given to few. Coming home though bent and bias for the sake of why so. Awkward as I am. Here and there invincible things as they are.

I write quietly to her. She is a figure of other as thin as paper.

Sorrow for uproar and wrongs of this world. You covenant to love.

* * *

EMILY DICKINSON:

Master.
　　　If you saw a bullet
hit a Bird—and he told you
he was'nt shot—you might weep
at his courtesy, but you would
certainly doubt his word—

(ML 32)

If history is a record of survivors, Poetry shelters other voices.

Dickinson, Melville, Thoreau, and Hawthorne guided me back to what I once thought was the distant seventeenth century. Now I know that the arena in which Scripture battles raged among New Englanders with originary fury is part of our current American system and events, history and structure.

GOODWIFE WILLOWS: Then I had a mind for New England and I thought I should know more of my own heart. So I came and thought I saw more than ever I could have believed that I wondered earth swallowed me not up. And 25 Matthew 5—foolish virgins saw themselves

> void of all grace. I thought I was so and was gone no farther. And questioned all that ever the Lord had wrought, I'll never leave thee. I could now apprehend that yet desired the Lord not to leave me nor forsake me and afterward I thought I was now discovered. Yet hearing He would not hide His face forever, was encouraged to seek. But I felt my heart rebellious and loathe to submit unto Him. (C 151)

An English relation of conversion spoken at a territorial edge of America is deterritorialized and deterred by anxiety crucial to iconoclastic Puritan piety. Inexplicable acoustic apprehension looms over assurance and sanctification, over soil subsoil sea sky.

Each singular call. As the sound is the sense is. Severed on this side. Who would know there is a covenant. In a new world morphologies are triggered off.

* * *

Under the hammer of God's word (W 1:92).

During the 1630s and 1640s a mother tongue (English) had to find ways to accommodate new representations of reality. Helplessness and suffering caused by agrarian revolution in England, and changing economic structures all across Europe, pushed members of various classes and backgrounds into new collectivities. For a time English Protestant sects were united in a struggle against Parliament, the Jacobean and Stuart courts, the Anglican church, and Archbishop Laud. Collective resistance to political and religious persecution pushed particular groups to a radical separatism. Some sects broke loose from the European continent. Their hope was to ride out the cry and accusation of kingdoms of Satan until God would be all in all.

THOMAS SHEPARD: And so, seeing I had been tossed from the south to the north of England and now could go no farther, I then began to listen to a call to New England. (GP 55)

Schismatic children of Adam thought they were leaving the "wilderness of the world" to find a haven free of institutional structures they had united *against*. They were unprepared for the variability of directional change the wilderness they reached represented. Even John Winthrop complained of "our wildernes troubles in our first plantings" (AC 201).

A Bible, recently translated into the vernacular, was owned by nearly every member of the Bay Colony. It spoke to readers and nonreaders and signified the repossession of the Word by English. The Old and New Testaments, in English, were indispensable fictive realities connecting the emigrants to a familiar State-form and to home. Though they crossed a wide and northern ocean, Scripture encompassed them.

From the first, Divinity was knotted in Place. If the Place was found wanting, and it was by many, a rhetoric had to be double-knotted to hold perishing absolutism safe. First-generation leaders of this hegira to new England tied themselves and their followers to a dialectical construction of the American land as a virgin garden preestablished for them by the Author and Finisher of creation.

"Come to me and you shall find rest unto your souls."

To be released from bonds . . . absorbed into catastrophe of pure change.

"Flee, save your lives, and be like the heath in the wild."

Here is unappropriated autonomy. Uncounted occupied space. No covenant of King and people. No centralized State. Heavy pressure of finding no content. Openness of the breach.

"The gospel is a glass to show men the face of God in Christ. . . . The law is that glass that showeth a man his own face, and what he himself is. Now if this glass be taken away . . ." (W 1:74).

WIDOW ARRINGTON: Hearing Dr. Jenison, Lamentations 3—let us search and turn to the Lord—which struck my heart as an arrow. And it came as a light into me and the more the text was opened more I saw my heart. And hearing that something was lost when God came for searching. And when I came I durst not tell my husband fearing he would loath me if he knew me. And I resolved none should know nor I would tell. (C 184–85)

* * *

On October 3, 1635, Thomas Shepard and his family arrived in Boston Harbor on the ship *Defense*. "Oh, the depth of God's grace here," he later wrote, "that when he [man] deserves nothing else but separation from God, and to be driven up and down the world as a vagabond or as dried leaves, fallen from our God . . ." (GP 14).

There is a direct relation between sound and meaning.

Early spiritual autobiographies in America often mean to say that a soul has found love in what the Lord has done. "Oh, that when so many come near to mercy, and fall short of it, yet me to be let in! Caleb and Joshua to be let into Canaan, when they rest so near, and all perish" (W 2:229). Words sound other ways. I hear short-circuited conviction. Truth is stones not bread. The reins are still in the hands of God. He has set an order but he is not tied to that order. Sounds touch every coast and corner. He will pick out the vilest worthy never to be beloved. There is no love. I am not in the world where I am.

In his journal, Mr. Shepard wrote: "To heal this wound, which was but skinned over before, of secret atheism and unbelief" (GP 135).

* * *

Finding is the First
Act (MBED 1043)

After the beaver population in New England had been decimated by human greed, when roads were cut through unopened countryside, the roadbuilders often crossed streams on abandoned beaver dams, instead of taking time to construct wooden bridges. When other beaver dams collapsed from neglect, they left in their wake many years' accumulation of dead bark, leaves, twigs, and silt. Ponds they formed disappeared with the dams, leaving rich soil newly opened to the sun. These old pond bottoms, often many acres wide, provided fertile agricultural land. Here grass grew as high as a person's shoulder. Without these natural meadows many settlements could not have been established as soon as they were.

Early narratives of conversion and first captivity narratives in New England are often narrated by women. A woman, afraid of not speaking well, tells her story to a man who writes it down. The participant reporters follow and fly out of Scripture and each other. All testimonies are bereft, brief, hungry, pious, *authorized.*

Shock of God's voice speaking English.

Sound moves over the chaos of place in people. In this hungry world anyone may be eaten. What a nest and litter. A wolf lies coiled in the lamb.

Silence becomes a Self. Open your mouth.

In such silence women were talking. Undifferentiated powerlessness swallowed them. When did the break at this degree of distance happen?

Silence calls me himself. Open your mouth.

Whosoever. Not found written in the book of life.

During a later Age of Reason eighteenth-century Protestant gentlemen signed the Constitution in the city of Philadelphia. These first narratives from wide-open places re-place later genial totalities.

During the 1850s, when the Republic was breaking apart, newly exposed soil from abandoned narratives was as rich and fresh as a natural meadow.

Emily Dickinson and Herman Melville are bridge builders. Their writing vaults the streams. They lead me in nomad spaces. They sieve cipherings, hesitations, watchings, survival of sound-meaning associations: the hound and cry, track and call. So much strangeness from God. What is saved to be said.

Once dams, narratives are bridges.

In 1850, when Melville wrote about American literary expression, he called the essay "Hawthorne and His Mosses" and chose a fragment from Hawthorne's story of Puritan doubt.

" 'Faith!' shouted Goodman Brown, in a voice of agony and desperation; and the echoes of the forest mocked him, crying—'Faith! Faith!' as if bewildered wretches were seeking her all through the wilderness" (PT 251).

* * *

THOMAS SHEPARD:

> *Object*. But Christ is in heaven; how can I receive him and his love?
>
> *Ans*. A mighty prince is absent from a traitor; he sends his herald with a letter of love, he gives it him to read; how can he receive the love of the prince when absent? *Ans*. He sees his love in his letter, he knows it came from him, and so at a distance closeth with him by this means; so here, he that was dead, but now is alive, writes, sends to thee; O, receive his love here in his word; this is receiving "him by faith." (W 2:599–600)

In Europe, Protestant tradition since Luther had maintained that no one could fully express her sins. In New England, for some reason hard to determine, Protestant strictures were reversed. Bare promises were insufficient. Leaders and followers had to voice the essential mutability they suddenly faced. Now the minister's scribal hand copied down an applicant for church membership's narrative of mortification and illumination.

In *The Puritan Conversion Narrative: The Beginnings of American Expression*, Patricia Caldwell points out that during the 1630s, in the Bay Colony, a disclaimer about worthlessness and verbal inadequacy had to be followed by a verbal performance strong enough to convince the audience-congregation of the speaker's sincerity.

New England's first isolated and independent clerics must have wrestled with many conflicting impulses and influences. Rage against authority and rage for order, desire for union with the Father and the guilty knowledge they had abandoned their own mothers and fathers. In the 1630s a new society was being shaped or shaping itself. Oppositional wreckers and builders considered themselves divine instruments committed to the creation of a holy commonwealth. In 1636 the antinomian controversy erupted among this "Singular Prospect of Churches erected in an *American* Corner of the World, on purpose to express and pursue the Protestant *Reformation*" (MC 172).

The antinomian controversy circled around a woman, Anne Hutchinson, and what was seen to be "the Flewentess of her Tonge and her Willingness to open herselfe and to divulge her Opinions and to sowe her seed in us that are but highway side and Straynger to her" (AC 353). Thomas Shepard made this accusation. Paradoxically, he was one of the few ministers who required women to recite their confessions of faith publicly, before the gathered congregation. Hugh Peter lectured Anne Hutchinson in court: "You have stept out of your place, *you have rather bine a Husband than a Wife and a preacher than a Hearer; and a Magistrate than a Subject.* And soe you have thought to carry all Thinges in Church and Commonwealth, as you would and have not bine humbled for this" (AC 382–83).

Peter, Cotton, Winthrop, Eliot, Wilson, Dudley, Shepard, and other men had stepped out of their places when they left England. She was humbled by them for their Transgression. Anne Hutchinson was the community scapegoat. "The Mother Opinion of all the rest. . . . From the womb of this *fruitful opinion*, and from the countenance here by given to immediate and unwarranted revelations, 'tis not easie to relate how many monsters, worse than African, arose in these regions of *America*: But a *synod* assembled at *Cambridge*, whereof Mr. Shepard was no small part, most happily crushed them all" (M 1:386).

NOAH WEBSTER:

SCĀPE′-GŌAT, *n.* [*escape* and *goat*] In *the Jewish ritual*, a goat which was brought to the door of the tabernacle, where the high priest laid his hands upon him, confessing the sins of the people, and putting them on the head of the goat; after which the goat was sent into the wilderness, bearing the iniquities of the people. *Lev.*xvi. (WD 986)

Kenneth Burke says, in *A Grammar of Motives*, "Dialectic of the Scapegoat": "When the attacker chooses for himself the object of attack, it is usually his blood brother; the debunker is much closer to the debunked than others are; Ahab was pursued by the white whale he was pursuing" (GM 406–7).

René Girard says, in *The Scapegoat*, "What is a Myth?": "Terrified as they [the persecutors] are by their own victim, they see themselves as completely passive, purely reactive, totally controlled by this scapegoat at the very moment when they rush to his attack. They think that all initiative comes from him. There is only room for a single cause in their field of vision, and its triumph is absolute, it absorbs all other causality: it is the scapegoat" (S 43).

I say that the Scapegoat Dialectic and mechanism is peculiarly open to violence if the attacker is male; his bloodbrother, female. Kenneth Burke and René Girard dissect grammars and mythologies in a realm of discourse structured, articulated, and repeated by men.

THOMAS SHEPARD: We are all in Adam, as a whole country in a parliament man; the whole country doth what he doth. And although we made no particular choice of Adam to stand for us, yet the Lord made it for us; who, being goodness itself, bears more good will to man than he can or could bear to himself; and being wisdom itself, made the wisest choice, and took the wisest course for the good of man. (W 1:24)

* * *

A Short Story

GOVERNOR WINTHROP: She thinkes that the Soule is annihilated by the Judgement that was sentenced upon Adam. Her Error springs from her Mistaking of the Curse of God upon Adam, for that Curse doth not implye Annihilation of the soule and body, but only a dissolution of the Soule and Body.

MR. ELIOT: She thinks the Soule to be Nothinge but a Breath, and so vanisheth. I pray put that to her.

MRS. HUTCHINSON: *I thinke the soule to be nothing but Light* (AC 356).

* * *

The Erroneous Gentlewoman

GOVERNOR WINTHROP: We have thought good to send for you to understand how things are, that if you be in an erroneous way we may reduce you that so you may become a profitable member here among us. (AC 312)

THOMAS SHEPARD: I confes I am wholy unsatisfied in her Expressions to some of the Errors. Any Hereticke may bringe a slye Interpritation, upon any of thease Errors and yet hould them to thear Death: therfor I am unsatisfied. (AC 377)

ANNE HUTCHINSON: My Judgment is not altered though my Expression alters.

BROTHER WILLSON: Your Expressions, whan your Expressions are soe contrary to the Truth. (AC 378)

NOAH WEBSTER:

EX-PRES´SION, (eks-presh´un,) *n*. The act of expressing; the act of forcing out by pressure, as juices and oils from plants.

2. The act of uttering, declaring, or representing; utterance; declaration; representation; as, an *expression* of the public will. (WD 426)

MRS. HUTCHINSON: I doe not acknowledge it to be an Error but a Mistake. *I doe acknowledge my Expression to be Ironious but my Judgment was not Ironious*, for I held befor as you did but could not express it soe. (AC 361)

NOAH WEBSTER:

ER-RO´NE-OUS, *a*. [L.-*erroneus*, from *erro*, to err.]

1. Wandering; roving; unsettled.

They roam
Erroneous and disconsolate. *Philips*.

2. Deviating; devious; irregular; wandering from the right course.

Erroneous circulation of blood *Arbuthnot*. (WD 408)

ANNE HUTCHINSON: *So thear was my Mistake. I tooke Soule for Life*. (AC 360)

NOAH WEBSTER: Noah is here called *Man.* (WD xxiii)

* * *

A Woman's Delusion

A seashore where everything.

A tumult of mind.

Sackcloth and run up and down.

Every durable thread. Mediator. There is rebellion. A man cannot look. The sacrifice of Noah is a type. We dress our garden. There are properties. Proof must be guiding and leading.

Stooped so far.

Bruising lash of the law. Tender affections bear with the weak. An answerable wedge. But where is the work? Why is the church compared to a garden? We are dark ages and young beginners. Apprehending ourselves we want anything. These are words set down. Surfaces. Who has felt most mercy? Preaching to stone. A thin cold dangerous realm. Tidings. He appears. Anoint. Echoes and reverberations of love. Anoint. Washed and witnessing. Peter denies him. Anoint. Whole treasures of looks to the heart. It is one thing to trust to be saved. Selfpossession. She heard his question. Never thought of it. No thought today. Unapproachable December seems to be. The sun is a spare trope.

Shadow cast. Moment of recognition.

The conclusion of years can any force of intellect. That such ferocities are drowned by double act or immediate stroke. So much error. Old things done away. Name and that other in itself opposite.

Expression. I was born to make use of it. *Schism*. What is the reason of it? *Zeal*. An instance of our crime is blunder. *Object*. It may be a question. *Narration*. Can there be a better pattern? *Weary*. What do we imagine? *Swearing*. If I had time and was not mortal. But he. Scraps of predominance. *Answer*. So there is some grievance driven out of the way. *Objection*. Relation to the speaker. Speech to the wind. Particulars.

How shall I put on my coat?

Distance beyond comparison. Sleep between two.

* * *

This walker with God (M 1:390)

His name and office sweetly did agree,
Shepard by name, and in his ministry. (W 1:clxxix)

THOMAS SHEPARD: And I considered how unfit I was to go to such a good land with such an unmortified, hard, dark, formal, hypocritical heart. (GP 61)

Thomas Shepard was an evangelical preacher who comforted and converted many people: "as great a *converter* of *souls* as has ordinarily been known in our days" (M 1:380). Before he came to America, "although Mr. Shepard were but a young man, yet there was that *majesty* and *energy* in his preaching and that *holiness* in his life, which was not ordinary," said Cotton Mather in *Magnalia Christi Americana* (M 1:382). Edward Johnson called him "that gratious sweete Heavenly minded, and soule-ravishing Minister . . . in whose soule the Lord shed abroad his love so abundantly, that thousands of souls have cause to blesse God for him" (WWP 77). Thomas Prince said he "scarce ever preached a sermon but some-one or other of his congregation was struck in great distress and cried out in agony, 'What shall I do to be saved?' " (GP 8). Jonathan Mitchell remembered Shepard's Cambridge ministry: "*Unless it had been four years living in heaven, I know not how I could have more cause to bless God with wonder*" (C 13). Mitchell also recalled a day when "Mr. Shepard preached most profitably. That night I was followed with serious thoughts of my inexpressible misery, wherein I go on most miserably from Sabbath to Sabbath, without God, and without redemption" (M 2:85). Thomas Shepard called his longest spoken literary production, a series of sermons unpublished in his lifetime, *The Parable of the Ten Virgins Opened and Applied.* He married three times. Two wives died as a result of childbirth. His three sons, Thomas, Samuel, and Jeremiah, became ministers. The earnest persecutor of Anne Hutchinson and repudiator of "erroneous Antinomian doctrines" confided to his journal: "I have seen a God by reason and never been amazed at God. I have seen God himself and have been ravished to behold him" (GP 136). The author of *The Sound Believer* also told his diary: "On lecture morning this came into my thoughts, that the greatest part of a Christian's grace lies in mourning for the want of it" (GP 198).

Edward Johnson pictured the minister of the Cambridge First Church as a "poor, weak, pale-complexioned man" (GP 8) whose physical powers were feeble but spent to the full. He wept while composing his sermons and went up to the pulpit "as if he expected there to give up his account of his stewardship" (W I:clxxix). Mather called Shepard "Pastor Evangelicus." "Now, to take true measures of his conversation," the historian wrote, "one of the best glasses that can be used is the *diary*, wherein he did himself keep the remembrances of many remarkables that passed betwixt his *God* and *himself*; who were indeed *a suffient theatre to one another*" (M I:390).

When Thomas Shepard died after a short illness, August 25, 1649, he was forty-three. "Returning home from a council at Rowly, he fell into a *quinsie*, with a symptomatical fever, which suddenly stopped a *silver trumpet*, from whence the People of God had often heard *the joyful sound* (M I:386).

Some of his last words were "Lord, I am vile, but thou art righteous" (GP 237).

Cotton Mather described the character of his daily conversation as "*a trembling walk with god*" (M I:390).

* * *

} *S*:

THOMAS SHEPARD: thou wert in the dangers of the sea in thy mothers woombe then & see how god hath miraculously preserued thee, that thou art still aliue, & thy mother's woombe & the terrible seas haue not been thy graue. (*S* side of MB)

Probably sometime in 1646, Thomas Shepard wrote a brief autobiography entitled "T• { *My Birth & Life*: } S:" into one half of a small leather-bound pocket notebook. Theatrical pen strokes by the protagonist shelter and embellish the straightforward title that sunders his initials. Conversion is an open subject. Or is it a question of splitting the author's name from its frame of compositional expression.

The narrative begins with an energetic account of the author's birth "vpon the 5 day of Nouember, called the Powder treason day, & that very houre of the day wherin the Parlament should haue bin blown vp by Popish preists . . . which occasioned my father to giue me this name Thomas. Because he sayd I would hardly beleeue that euer any such wickednes should be attempted by men agaynst so religious & good Parlament" (CS 357). Seventy-four pages later (in the original manuscript) the autobiography breaks off abruptly, as it began, with calamity. This time the death in childbed of the author's second wife, here referred to by her husband, as "the eldest daughter of mr Hooker a blessed stock" (CS 391). Shepard married this eldest daughter of one of the most powerful theocrats in New England in 1637, the same year Mrs. Hutchinson was silenced. Unlike Mrs. Hutchinson, Mrs. Shepard was a woman of "incomparable meeknes of spirit, toward my selfe especially . . . being neither too lauish nor sordid in any thing so that I knew not what was vnder her hands" (CS 392). When she died, nine years and four male children later, "after 3 weekes lying in," two of her sons had predeceased her. On her deathbed this paragon of feminine piety and humility "continued praying vntil the last houre of her death: . . . Ld tho I vnwoorthy Ld on woord on woord &c. & so gaue vp the ghost, thus ——

god hath visited me & scourged me for my sins & sought to weane me fro this woorld, but I haue euer found it a difficult thing to pfit euer but a little by sorest & sharpest afflictions;" (CS 392–93, with spacing of original MS).

"T• { *My Birth & Life*: } S:" is littered with the deaths of mothers. The loss of his own mother when Shepard was a small child could never be settled.

Creation implies separation. The last word of "T• { *My Birth & Life*: } S:" is "afflictions."

Eighty-six blank manuscript pages emphasize this rupture in the pious vocabulary of order. The reader reads empty paper.

The absence of a definitive conclusion to Shepard's story of his life and struggles is a deviation from the familiar Augustinian pattern of self-revelation used by other English nonconformist Reformers.

Allegoria and *historia* should be united in "T• {*My Birth & Life*:} S:" Doubting Thomas should transcend the empirical events of his times to become the figura of the Good Shepard, but the repetitive irruption of death into life is mightier than this notion of enclosure.

"Woe to those that keep silent about God," as Kenneth Burke paraphrases St. Augustine, "for where he is concerned, even the talkative are as though speechless" (RR 53). "Silence reveals speech—unless it is speech that reveals silence," Pierre Macherey has written in *A Theory of Literary Production* (TP 86).

State of the manuscript. *Leaves that stood.* Labor of elaboration. He is the god. A word is the beginning of every Conversion.

The purpose of editing is to reach the truth.

Mr. Shepard's manuscript is a draft. Shortcomings and error. The minister made no revisions in this unsettled account of his individual existence. Rational corrections by editors lie in wait. *Leaf of the story*. Distortion will begin in the place of flight.

THOMAS SHEPARD: He is the god who tooke me vp when my own mother dyed who loued me, & wn my stepmother cared not for me, & wn lastly my father also dyed & foorsooke me w^{n} I was yong & little & could take no care for my selfe. (*T* side of MB)

* * *

T• {

Is it not hence؟

(*T* side of MB)

There is no title on the binding of the notebook that contains the manuscript. The paper is unlined. There are no margins. There is no front or back. You can open and shut it either way. Over time it has been used in multiple ways by Shepard and by others. Thomas Shepard, its first owner, used both ends of the book to begin writing.

Each side holds a personal history in reverse. On one side, I have here called *S*, is the uninterrupted interrupted *Autobiography*.

Then there is the empty center.

But I can turn the book over so that side *S* is inverted and begin to read another narrative by the same author. Now the protagonist's more improvisational commentary decenters the premeditated literary production of "T• { *My Birth & Life*: } S:" Subjects are chosen then dropped. Messages are transmitted and hidden. Whole pages have been left open. Another revelation or problem begins with a different meaning or purpose. Although dates occur on either side, it is unclear which side was written first.

We might call the creation on this side an understudy. I will call this *T* side "An Inside Narrative."

Then there is the empty center.

* * *

with honey within, with oil in public:

God's Plot: The Paradoxes of Puritan Piety, Being the Autobiography & Journal of Thomas Shepard (1972), edited and with an introduction by Michael McGiffert, is now the standard reference for reading this text.

McGiffert, who tells us he restored some of the blunt vocabulary that had been expunged by two genteel nineteenth-century editors, overlooked the structural paradox of the material object whose handwritten pages he laboriously and faithfully transcribed. McGiffert's is the fourth edition of Shepard's *Autobiography*. An earlier verbatim text was edited by Allyn Bailey Forbes for the Colonial Society of Massachusetts, *Publications*, volume 27 (*Transactions*, 1927–1930). Both editors included sections from the *T* side of the manuscript book in their editions. Forbes called the sections "random notes" and placed them last, under the title "Appendix." McGiffert also put them last, under the heading: "The following material consists of notes written by Shepard in the manuscript of the *Autobiography*." Neither editor saw fit to point out the fact that Shepard left two manuscripts in one book separated by many pages and positioned so that to read one you must turn the other upside down.

Both editors deleted something from each history. McGiffert decided the financial transactions on side *S* were of no autobiographical importance. Forbes included them but buried Shepard's hostile reference to John Cotton on side *T* in a footnote to side *S*. Shepard placed this cryptic list of accusations against his fellow Saint alone on the recto side of leaf 3. Far from being "random" or a footnote, the list provides a vivid half-smothered articulation of New England's savage intersectine Genesis. Possibly the Colonial Society of Massachusetts balked at displaying this ambiguous sample of colonial ideology.

Mr Cotton: repents not: but is hid only

1: W^{n} M^{ris} Hutchinsō was conuented he commeded
her for all that shee did before her confinement
& so gaue her a light to escape thorow the
crowd w^{t} honour,

2: being askt whether all reulations were lost
bec: all reuelations were either to compleat
Scripture or for the infancy of the weake
church,
he answered that they were all ceased about
ptic. euents; rules to weake X^{tians}; & seemd
to confirme it now: ~~///~~ whereas in the sermō
it was to weake church vnder the old
testament, he did extend it to weake
X^{tians} also vnder the new;

> 3: he doth stiffly hold the reuelatiō of or good
> estate still, without any sight of woord
> or woorks: / (CS 386*n*, MB 3)

Here is the correct order of the sections written by Shepard in side *T*, or "An Inside Narrative":

> 1. A Roman being asked.
> 2. Mr. Cotton: repents not: but is hid only.
> 3. Law. that the magistrate kisse the Churchs
> feet: that h: meddle n^t. beyond his bounds,
> 4. My Life: Lord Jesu pdō: / euery day.
> 5. April: 4 1639: prep: for a
> fast.
> 6. Is it not hence?
> 7. An: 1639 / The good things I have received
> of the Lord:
>
> (MB, GP, CS)

Shepard's list of "The good things I haue receiued of the Lord" has fourteen sections and continues for eight pages. The nonconformist minister meant to give praise and thanksgiving to God, but images of panic, haste, and abandonment disunite the Visible and Spiritual.

The Lord is the Word. He scatters short fragments. Jonah cried out to the Word when floods encompassed him. A Sound Believer hears old Chaos as in a deep sea. A narrative refuses to conform to its project.

Side *S* ends abruptly with afflictions sent by God to "scourge" the author. Side *T* also breaks off suddenly. The author is remembering his earlier ministry in Earles Colne, "a most prophane" English town. "Here the Lord kept me fro troubles 3 yeares & a halfe vntill the Bishop Laud put me to silence & would not let me liue in the town & this he did w^n I looked to be made a shame & confusiō to all:" (CS 395).

From confusion in old England to affliction in new England. Problematical type and antitype. Everything has its use.

:/

> not knowing that I shall
> liue to tell them my selfe
> with my own mouth (CS 352, MB)

Some of the eighty-six blank manuscript pages separating *T* and *S* have been written on since, by various mediaries. All of these men see a higher theme to side *S*. They follow its trajectory as if side *T* were an eccentric inversion. Their additions form a third utterance of authority in the Sincere Convert's transitory division of *T* from *S* (life from birth).

On the second leaf (r) of side *T*, or "An Inside Narrative," Mr. Shepard wrote down a single citation of discord.

> A Roman, being asked how he liud
> so long—answered—intus melle, foris
> oleo: /
>
> quid loquac*ius* vanitate, ait augustinus.
> (*T* side of MB, italics mine)

Forbes had the discretion to stay away from translating the garbled Latin in his interpretation of the minister's script. "A Roman being asked how he liud so long. answered intus melle, foris oleo: quid loquacior, vanitate, ait augustinus" (CS 397). McGiffert agreed with Forbes's transcription and proceeded to offer the following translation: "On the inside, honey; on the outside, oil. Which babbled more of vanity?, said Augustine" (GP 77*n*). But McGiffert's transcription of the Latin *quid* and *loquacior* cannot agree with one another; moreover, there is nothing in the Latin to justify the word *babbled*.

A more exact reading of the enigmatic passage would be: "With honey within; with oil in public: What is more garrulous than vanity, said Augustine."

We will never know if this entry refers to John Cotton, Thomas Shepard, or the human condition. It could be a questionable interpretation of any evangelical minister's profession. It could be a self-accusation or a reference to John Cotton's preaching. It could be a note for a sermon or merely a sign that the author knows St. Augustine.

In the seventeenth century the word *oil*, used as a verb, often meant "to anoint." The holy oil of religious rites.

Five foolish virgins took their lamps but forgot the oil for trimming. They went to meet the bridegroom. The door was shut against them. "I say unto you I know you not."

To *oil* one's tongue meant, and still means, to adopt or use flattering speech. "Error, oiled with obsequiousness, . . . has often the Advantage of Truth.—1776" (OUD).

"*Their throat is an open sepulcher.* One may apply this verse to greed, which is often the motive behind men's deceitful flattery . . . for greed is insatiably openmouthed, unlike sepulchers which are sealed up" (St. Augustine, *Enarrationes* [AP 1:57]). "They that observe lying vanities forsake their own mercy" (Jonah, to God).

Alone on the second leaf the citation assumes its own mystery.

Shepard's epigraph, if it is an epigraph to side *T*, or "An Inside Narrative," is a dislocation and evocative contradiction in the structure of this two-sided book that may or may not be a literary work.

In 1819, James Blake Howe turned the book upside down, probably to conform with the direction of the *Autobiography*, and inscribed his own name, place of residence, and the date on the same page.

* * *

MR. PRINCE: Though [Shepard's] voice was low, yet so searching was his preaching, so great a power attending, as a hypocrite could not easily bear it, & it seemed almost irresistable. (*S* side of MB)

* * *

Divers

Mat

In this setdown the ques
tion of C's desiples
why they asks him
not men ought sometimes to
askes questions patiently where
they hear the word upon
sum occasion
(*written in another hand in* T *side of* MB)

The des thought at the
(*written in another hand on a page in* T *side of* MB)

* * *

Study in Logology

COTTON MATHER: The name of COTTON is as an ointment poured forth. (M 1:270)

NOAH WEBSTER: Oil is an unctuous substance expressed or drawn from various animal and vegetable substances. The distinctive characteristics of oil are inflammability, fluidity, and insolubility in water. Oils are fixed and greasy, fixed and essential, and volatile and essential. (WD 770)

KENNETH BURKE: Let us recall, for what it might be worth, that in his [St. Augustine's] treatise "On the Teacher" (*De Magistro*), a discussion with his son on the subject of what would now popularly be called "semantics," he holds that the word *verbum* is derived from a verb meaning "to strike" (*a verberando*)—and the notion fits in well with his references to the lash of God's discipline. See, for instance, *Confessions* (x, vi), where he says that he loves God because God had struck (*percussisti*) him with His Word. (RR 50)

BARBARA JOHNSON: And this is what makes the meaning of Melville's last work so *striking*. (CD 109)

* * *

Fly-leaves

THOMAS SHEPARD: You have not only to deale with a Woman this day that houlds diverse erronius Opinions but with one that never had any trew Grace in her hart and that by her owne Tenect. Yea this day she hath shewed herselfe to be a Notorius Imposter, it is a Tricke of as notorious Subtiltie as ever was held in the Church, to say thear is no Grace in the Saints and now to say she hath, and that she all this while hath not altered her Judgment, but only her Expressions. (AC 383)

* * *

THOMAS SHEPARD
Anagram: More hath pass'd
(W 3:515)

At the time of the antinomian controversy Thomas Shepard preached his series of sermons around Matthew 25: 1–13, called *The Parable of the Ten Virgins Opened and Applied.* These sermons were first published in 1659 by Jonathan Mitchell, minister at Cambridge, and Thomas Shepard, son of the author, "for the common benefit of the Lord's people from the author's own notes."

Between 1637 and 1640, Thomas Shepard transcribed into another leatherbound pocket notebook, containing 190 pages, the testimonies of faith given in his church by fifty-one men and women who were applying for church membership. If you turn it upside down and read the other way, thirty-three pages of the little volume are crammed with his notes from the sermons of four ministers, including John Cotton. These sermon notes are immediately followed by two of the testimonies, one of them anonymous. Shepard later said of 1637 that God in that year alone "delivered the country from war with the Indians and Familists, who rose and fell together" (W 1:cxxvi).

During the early seventeenth century it was the custom for churchgoers to copy down sermons as they were being spoken and to discuss them later, in detail, at home. In England the Puritan habit of taking notes during the service impressed foreigners. Did Thomas copy these doubting testimonies of faith while he was listening, or did the author of *The Sound Believer, The Sincere Convert, Discovering the small number of True Believers, Of Ineffectual Hearing of the Word*, and *The Clear Sunshine of the Gospel Breaking Upon The Indians In New England; or, An Historical Narration*, among other spoken or written literary productions, recompose these confessions?

* * *

SHOWING THAT THERE IS A VAST DIFFERENCE BETWIXT A SINCERE CHRISTIAN AND THE CLOSEST HYPOCRITE (W 2:206)

Voices are trimming their lamps.

Close and I will carry you. If sanctification and expression are joined together; the I is a public election. These narrators are chosen. Hypocrite grace? The Pastor's doubt infiltrates each voice. Apprehension invades writing. "If no hope in this life, of all men most miserable; some young ones think it is too soon; old men that are near do it; many have businesses, and can not; can not you carry it to the fields . . . ?" (W 2:635) After Shepard, what is the truth? We cannot know. Approach is of little use to them. Each autopresentation signals him.

"Of the desire of grace that may be in hypocrites. *Give us of your oil etc.*" (w 2:465).

"*Our Lamps are out*" (w 2:458).

Print beats imagination back.

Words are slippery. Questions of audience, signature, self and other will be answered later by historians, genealogists, graphologists, handwriting experts, who need to produce a certain rationalism for this unstable I-witnessing, uncovering relation. Can all of the professional intermediaries ever since reimagine this finite–infinite commingling communion?

Trammels of identity. Revelation approaches as a mystery.

* * *

The Visible Church

Authorities in the academic study of American literature have decided that a candidate for membership in the congregation of the Church of Christ in Cambridge in New England had been carefully screened by the church elders before he or she presented a personal "confession and declaration of God's manner of working on the soul" in public. Apparently, candidates had to settle private accusations against them and present private testimonies first. Sometimes the preliminary screening process took months. After a person had been cleared by the church authorities, he or she delivered the public confession, usually during the weekday meeting. The congregation then voted by a show of hands, and their decision was supposed to be unanimous. During Sunday service an applicant was finally accepted into church fellowship.

George Selement and Bruce Woolley, editors for the *Collections of the Colonial Society*, say that the applicants, during this tumultuous time when it seemed dangerous to speak at all, especially to express spiritual enthusiasm, were from a wide social spectrum. A third could read or write. Almost half of recorded testimonies were from women. The speakers included four servants, two Harvard graduates, traders, weavers, carpenters, coopers, glovers, and one sailor. Most were concerned with farming and with acquisition of property. Most applicants were in their twenties, some in their forties. Most were starting to raise families. Elizabeth Cutter and Widow Arrington were in their sixties. Each person knew that reception into church fellowship was necessary in order to gain economic and social advantage in the community. Some later became rich; some are untraceable now through genealogical records. Both male servants who spoke gained financial and political freedom.

Two women in Shepard's notebook were servants. Genealogical trace of them has vanished with their surnames. Two applicants were widows who managed their own estates. The rest generally spent their days cleaning, sewing, marketing, cooking, farming, and giving birth to, then caring for, children. Some later died in childbirth. Mrs. Sparhawk died only a month after Shepard recorded her narrative. Some survived their husbands by many years.

Thomas Hooker, who became Shepard's father-in-law in 1637 and was the previous minister of the Cambridge parish, moved to Connecticut partly because he felt the colony's admission procedures were too harsh. Hooker insisted that confessions by women should be read aloud in public by men. Governor Winthrop, in his *History of New England*, citing feminine "feebleness" and "shamefac't modesty and melanchollick fearfulness," preferred that women's "relations" remain private; a male elder should read them before a select committee. Shepard and one or two other ministers felt differently. "The Confessions of diverse propounded to be received & were entertained as members" shows that although Shepard thought women should defer to their husbands in worldly matters, in his theology of conversion they were relatively independent. These narratives reflect this autonomy. Some are as long or longer than those spoken by men.

* * *

THOMAS SHEPARD

Anagram: Arm'd as the shop

(W 3:515)

Notes written in the minister's hand on the flyleaf of the other, sermon side of the manuscript he titled "The Confessions of diverse propounded to be received & were entertained as members":

1. You say some brethren cannot live comfortably with so little.

2. We put all the rest upon a temptation. Lots being but little, and estates will increase or live in beggary. For to lay land out far off is intolerable to men; near by, you kill your cattle.

3. Because if another minister come, he will not have room for his company—Religion—.

4. Because now, if ever, is the most fit season; for if gate be opened, many will come in among us, and fill all places, and no room in time to come; at least, not such good room as now. And now you may best sell.

5. Because Mr. Vane will be upon our skirts. (GP 90)

* * *

MATT. xviii: 11—"I came to save that which was lost" (W 1:111).

Each confession of faith is an eccentric, concentrated improvisation and arrest. Each narrator's proper name forms a chapter heading. Wives and servants are property. Their names are appropriated for masculine consistency.

Goodman Luxford His Wife
Brother Collins His Wife
Brother Moore His Wife
Brother Greene His Wife
Brother Parish's Wife
Brother Crackbone His Wife
The Confession of John Sill His Wife
John Stedman His Wife's Confession
Brother Jackson's Maid

Written representation of the Spirit is sometimes ineffectual, words only images or symbols of the clear sunshine of the Gospel. "Go to a painted sun, it gives you no heat, nor cherishith you not. So it is here, etc." Often the minister surrounds a name with ink scrawls and flourishes.

Flights or freezes. Proof and chaos. Immanent sorrow of one, incomplete victory of another. *Use*, oh my unbelief.

Confessions are copied down quickly. Translinguistic idiosyncrasies imply but block consistency. A sound block will not be led. Mistaken biblical quotations are transcribed and abandoned. As the sound is, the sense is. Few revisions civilize verbal or visual hazards and webs of unsettled sanctification. The minister's nearly microscopic handwriting is difficult to decipher. He uses a form of shorthand in places.

A wild heart at the word shatters scriptural figuration.

Once again, by correcting, deleting, translating, or interpreting the odd symbols and abbreviated signals, later well-meaning editors have effaced the disorderly velocity of Mr. Shepard's evangelical enthusiasm.

For readability.

* * *

Writing speed of thought moving through dominated darkness (the privation) toward an irresistible confine possibly becoming woman.

The Soul's Immediate Closing with the Person (W 2:111)

BARBARY CUTTER: The Lord let me see my condition by nature out of 16 of Ezekiel and by seeing the holiness of the carriage of others about, her friends, and the more she looked on them the more she thought ill of herself. She embraced the motion to New England. Though she went through with many miseries and stumbling blocks at last removed and sad passages by sea. And after I came hither I saw my condition more miserable than ever. (C 89–90)

A Narrator-Scribe-Listener-Confessor-Interpreter-Pastor-Judge-Reporter-Author quickly changes person, character, country, and gender. Walk darkly here. This is to cross Scripture. These words are questions. Compel them to come in when Jonah is cast out of sight.

He singles them out.

His spirit comes home to them quiet as an ark above waters; rest and provender being desire to lay under Lord. Praying for him and hearing. Words drift together. Washed from her heart. Many foolish pray from the mouth. Some are condemned. Blossoms fly up as dust. He will not leave. Death cannot. "In favor is life." This outline is extracted. Now you will have him. She calls him so.

Some are asleep. Ten virgins trim their lamps.

My house is a waste. To doctrine to reason cry peace peace. This is that which fills a man. For this long ago Corinthians, Philippians, Thessalonians: motives differ. We are his people we stumble. What a wandering path confinement is when angels had not fallen. Pale clarity of day. Why no heart. Iniquities are not all I might

"Five were wise and five were foolish."

Once the doors were shut, these virgins were surely kept out. Glimpses.

Explication. What is acceptable? Toother. Miswritten he thought. He thought. Other redundancies. Reduced to lower case these words are past. To the supposed sepulcher. Purest virgin churches and professors, they took their lamps. What can we do? Prevail again? Against what do we watch?

Fiery law and tabernacles I beat the air.
Therefore as her and distancing.

* * *

"*Went forth to meet the Bridegroom.*" (W 2:111)

OLD GOODWIFE CUTTER:
I desired to come this way in sickness time
and Lord brought us through many sad troubles by sea
and when I was here the Lord rejoiced my heart.
But when come I had lost all and no comfort
and hearing from foolish virgins
those that sprinkled with Christ's blood were unloved. (C 145)

JOHN SILL HIS WIFE:
Oft troubled since she came hither,
her heart went after the world and vanities
and the Lord absented Himself from her
so that she thought God had brought her hither on purpose
to discover her. (C 51)

GOODWIFE WILLOWS:
And when husband gone, I thought all I had was but a form
and I went to Mr. Morton
and desired he would tell me how it was with me.
He told me if I hated that form
it was a sign I had more than a form. (C 150)

BROTHER WINSHIP'S WIFE:
Hearing 2 Jeremiah 14—two evils broken cisterns—
I was often convinced by Mr. Hooker my condition was miserable
and took all threatenings to myself. . . .
And I heard He that had smitten He could heal Hosea 6. . . .
Hearing—say to them that be fearful in heart, behold He comes—
Mr. Wells—pull off thy soles off thy feet for ground is holy.
And hearing Exodus 34, forgiving iniquity,

I thought Lord could will, was He willing. . . .
Hearing whether ready for Christ at His appearing
had fears, city of refuge. . . .
Hearing—oppressed undertake for me—eased. (C 147–49)

HANNAH BREWER:
And I heard that promise proclaimed—Lord, Lord merciful and gracious etc.—
but could apply nothing. (C 141)

BROTHER WINSHIP'S WIFE:
Hearing of Thomas' unbelief,
he showed trust in Lord forever
for there is everlasting strength and stayed. (C 149)

GOODWIFE USHER:
And I heard—come to me you that be weary—
and Lord turn me and I shall be turned—
and so when I desired to come hither
and found a discontented heart
and mother dead and my heart overwhelmed.
And I heard of a promise—fear not I'll be with thee.
And in this town I could not understand anything was said,
I was so blind, and heart estranged from people of people. (C 183)

MRS. SPARHAWK:
And then that place fury is not in me,
let Him take hold of my strength. . . .
And she
there was but two ways either to stand out
or take hold,
and saw the promise
and her
own insufficiency so to do. . . .
and mentioning a Scripture,
was asked whether she had assurance.
She said no but some hope. (C 68–69)

JOHN STEDMAN HIS WIFE:
Hearing Mr. Cotton out of Revelation—

Christ with a rainbow on his head, Revelation 10—
I thought there was nothing for me.
I thought I was like the poor man at the pool. (C 105)

GOODWIFE GRIZZELL:
Hearing Mr. Davenport on sea—
he that hardened himself against the Lord could not prosper—
and I thought I had done so.
But then he showed it was continuing in it
and I considered though I had a principle against faith
yet a kingdom divided cannot stand. (C 188–89)

WIDOW ARRINGTON:
And in latter end that sermon
there was obedience of sons and servants
then I thought—would I know?
And I thought Lord gave me a willing heart, etc.
And they that have sons can cry—Abba—Father,
and so have some stay
and I wished I had a place in wilderness to mourn. (C 185–86)

BROTHER JACKSON'S MAID:
When Christ was to depart nothing broke their heart so much as then. (C 121)

* * *

Walking alone in the fields

These first North American Inside Narratives cross the wide current of Scripture. I meet them in the fields. They show me what rigor. I dare not pity. When she went to meet the Bridegroom it was too early. Then there is nothing to believe. Scholars of the world, then there is no authority at all.

The iron face of filial systems.

The colonies of America break out.

Consider the parable of these wise and foolish virgins. They went to work to trim their lamps. What did the foolish say to the wise? That there is no difference? What a crossing. All their thoughts and searching. Is that what love is? Bewildered by history did they see iniquity? Did they spend whole days and nights trimming? When was the filth wiped off?

People of His pasture, does this give peace?

Sheep of His hand, is this the temptation of the place?

Mountains are interrupted by mountains. Planets are not fixed. They run together. Planets are globes of fire. Imagination is a lens. Pastness. We find by experience. A sentence tumbles into thought. A disturbance calls itself free.

* * *

At York Court, dined with the Judges, and spent the Evening at Ritchies with Bradbury and Hale of Portsmouth, a sensible young Lawyer. Bradbury says there is no need of Dung upon your Mowing Land if you dont feed it in the Fall nor Spring. Let the old Fog remain upon it, and die and rot and be washed into the Ground, and dont suffer your Cattle to tread upon it and so poach and break the soil, and you will never want any Dung.

—*Diary* of John Adams, Tuesday, June 25, 1771

Economy

Recipe to make Manure.

Take the Soil and Mud, which you cutt up and throw out when you dig Ditches in a Salt Marsh, and put 20 Load of it in a heap. Then take 20 Loads of common Soil or mould of Upland and Add to the other. Then to the whole add 20 Loads of Dung, and lay the whole in a Heap, and let it lay 3 months, then take your Spades And begin at one End of the Heap, and dig it up and throw it into another Heap, there let it lie, till the Winter when the Ground is frozen, and then cart it on, to your English Grass Land. . . . If I can so fence and secure Deacon Belchers and Lt. Belchers Orchards, as not to feed them at all in the Fall, Winter, nor Spring I could get a fine Crop of English Hay from thence. But I must keep up my Fences all Winter to keep off my Neighbours Creatures, Hog, Horses, Oxen, Cows and Sheep (JA 41).

* * *

This our erroneous gentlewoman. (M 2:516)

Thomas Hutchinson, Anne Hutchinson's great-great-grandson, is an interesting figure. Besides being the author of *The History of the Colony and Province of Massachusetts-Bay* (1765), still one of the most valuable histories of the early colonial period, he was the last royal governor of the province of Massachusetts. On August 26, 1765, when he was serving as both chief justice and lieutenant governor, an angry mob attacked his mansion. The rioters broke their way in with axes, smashed what they couldn't take, and stole, mutilated, or tossed away all of his books, including the manuscript of volume 1 of the *History* and a collection of documents he had been gathering for years as the basis of a public archive. Perhaps the original records of Anne Hutchinson's trial were lost in this tumult. According to historian Bernard Bailyn, this was the single most violent episode of resistance to the Stamp Act in Boston during the course of the American Revolution. Together with his preoriginal representation, Anne, Thomas Hutchinson was fated to serve as scapegoat for a new political opposition. Both were despised by founding fathers. John Winthrop loathed Anne; John Adams loathed Thomas. Thomas was also banished from the colony, though he was banished for his conservatism. "My temper," Governor Hutchinson once wrote, "does not incline to enthusiasm" (OTH 17). Much to his regret, he died in England.

In *The History of the Colony and Province of Massachusetts-Bay*, Thomas Hutchinson introduces his ancestor this way:

> There came over with Mr. Cotton, or about the same time, Mr. Hutchinson, and his family, who had lived at Alford in the neighborhood of Boston. Mr. Hutchinson had a good estate and was of good reputation. His wife, as Mr. Cotton says, "was well-beloved, and all the faithful embraced her conference and blessed God for her fruitful discourses." After she came to New England, she was treated with respect, and much notice was taken of her by Mr. Cotton and other principal persons, and particularly by Mr. Vane the governor. Her husband served in the general court, several elections, as a representative for Boston, until he was excused at the desire of the church. So much respect seems to have increased her natural vanity. Countenanced and encouraged by Mr. Vane and Mr. Cotton, she advanced doctrines and opinions which involved the colony in disputes and contentions . . . and had like to have produced ruin both to church

and state. The vigilance of some, of whom Mr. Winthrop was the chief, prevented, and turned the ruin from the country upon herself and many of her family and particular friends. . . . Mrs. Hutchinson thought fit to set up a meeting of the sisters also, where she repeated the sermons preached the Lord's day before, adding her remarks and expositions. Her lectures made much noise, and sixty or eighty principal women attended them. (HMB 1:49–50)

Lawrence Shaw Mayo, the editor of the edition of the *History* published by Harvard University Press in 1936, seems to have been surprised by Hutchinson's harsh judgment of his notorious female ancestor. He added a footnote as if to reassure himself: "William Hutchinson (1586–1642) and his wife Anne (1590–1643) were the great-great-grandparents of Governor Thomas Hutchinson. This fact makes more remarkable the judicial attitude maintained by the Governor in his treatment of Mrs. Hutchinson in the narrative" (HMB 1:49).

"The career of his great-great-grandmother Anne fascinated and chilled him," says Bernard Bailyn in *The Ordeal of Thomas Hutchinson*, also published by the Harvard University Press (OTH 22).

* * *

Inclosures

1773 Apr. 24TH. SATURDAY.

I have communicated to Mr. Norton Quincy, and to Mr. Wibird the important Secret [purloined letters from Thomas Hutchinson to Thomas Whately]. They are as much affected, by it, as any others. Bone of our Bone, born and educated among us! Mr. Hancock is deeply affected, is determined in Conjunction with Majr. Hawley to watch the vile Serpent [Hutchinson], and his deputy Serpent Brattle.

The Subtilty, of this Serpent, is equal to that of the old one.

Aunt is let into the Secret, and is full of her Interjections! . . .

Fine, gentle Rain last night and this morning, which will lay a foundation for a crop of Grass.

My Men at Braintree have been building me a Wall, this Week against my Meadow. This is all the Gain that I make by my Farm to repay me my great expence. I get my Land better secured—and manured (JA 81).

1773. Ap. 25. SUNDAY.

Heard Dr. Chauncey in the Morning and Dr. Cooper in the Afternoon. Dr. Cooper was up[on] Rev. 12.9. And the great Dragon was cast out, that old Serpent called the Devil and Satan, which deceiveth the whole World: he was cast out into the Earth and his Angells were cast out with him. Q[uery]. Whether the Dr. had not some political Allusions in the Choice of this Text (JA 81).

* * *

A Defence of Property

1774. Feby. 28.

I purchased of my Brother, my fathers Homestead, and House where I was born. The House, Barn and thirty five acres of Land of which the Homestead consists, and Eighteen acres of Pasture in the North Common, cost me 440£. This is a fine addition, to what I had there before, of arable, and Meadow. The Buildings and the Water, I wanted, very much.

That beautifull, winding, meandering Brook, which runs thro this farm, always delighted me.

How shall I improve it? Shall I try to introduce fowl Meadow And Herds Grass, into the Meadows? or still better Clover and Herdsgrass?

I must ramble over it and take a View. The Meadow is a great Object—I suppose near 10 Acres of [it]—perhaps more—and may be made very good, if the Mill below, by overflowing it, dont prevent. Flowing is profitable, if not continued too late in the Spring.

This Farm is well fenced with Stone Wall against the Road, against Vesey, against Betty Adams's Children, vs. Ebenezer Adams, against Moses Adams, and against me.

The North Common Pasture has a numerous Growth of Red Cedars upon it, perhaps 1,000, which in 20 years if properly pruned may be worth a Shilling each. It is well walled all round (JA 87–88).

* * *

A Documentary History

B. WOODBRIDGE:

UPON THE TOMB OF THE MOST REVEREND MR. JOHN COTTON, LATE TEACHER OF THE CHURCH OF BOSTON IN NEW-ENGLAND.

A simple *serpent*, or serpentine *dove*,
Made up of wisdom, innocence and love:
Neatness embroider'd with *it self* alone,
And *civils canonized* in a gown;
Embracing old and young, and low and high,
Ethics Imbodyed in *divinity*. . . .
O, what a monument of glorious worth,
When, in a *new edition*, he comes forth,
Without *erratas*, may we think he'l be
In *leaves* and *covers* of eternity!

(M I:284)

NOAH WEBSTER: We read in the Scriptures, that God, when he had created man, "blessed them; and said to them, Be fruitful and multiply, and replenish the earth, and subdue it: and have dominion over the fish of the sea," &c. God afterward planted a garden, and placed in it the man he had made, with a command to keep it, and to dress it; and he gave him a rule of moral conduct, in permitting him to eat the fruit of every tree in the garden, except one, the eating of which was prohibited. We further read, that God brought to Adam the fowls and beasts he had made, and that Adam gave them names; and that when his female companion was made, he gave her a name (WD xxiii).

CRISPUS ATTUCKS: We brought the first dominions into view in all their branches. "It was a Savage feast, carnivorous Animals devouring their Pray" (JA 227).
The *Political Disquisitions* is some other book.
Hearing and seeing salvation conceive enough has been said and *e contra*

JOHN ADAMS: I saw [Governor Hutchinson] this Morning pass my Window in a Chariot with the Secretary. And by the Marching and Countermarching of Councillors, I suppose they have been framing a Proclamation, offering a Reward to discover the Persons, their Aiders,

Abettors, Counsellors and Consorters, who were concerned in the Riot last Night (JA 87).

COTTON MATHER: Peers of America and confusion in England already this as that for our own records. "I would gladly contrive some way to relate so important a story as that of her affairs, without mentioning of her name; and therefore I will cover it with a convenient *periphrasis*. Behold, reader,

Nulla fere causa est, in qua non faemina litem moverit.

This our erroneous gentlewoman, at her coming out of Lincolnshire in England unto New-England, upon pretence of religion, was well respected among the professors of *this* religion (M 2:516).

The other interpretation is to show a difference between virgins.

LORD SAY AND SEAL: So you are dead to act an attack on property. *Quest.* Where is life then? *Ans.* Not the husk law.

THOMAS HUTCHINSON: The prospect of returning to America and laying my bones in the land of my forefathers for four preceding generations and if I add the mother of W.H. it will make five, is less than it has ever been. God grant me a composed mind submissive to his will; and may I be thankful that I am not reduced to those straits, which many others who are banished are, and have been (LH 347).

JAMES SAVAGE: Nor can I forgive the slight use of these invaluable documents which is evinced by Mather, the unhappy author of Magnalia Christi Americana, who, in the hurry of composing that endless work, seems to have preferred useless quotations of worthless books, two or three centuries older, or popular and corrupt traditions, to the full matter and precise statement of facts, dates, principles, and motives, furnished by authentick history (WH 1:iv).

COTTON MATHER: I would have tried, whether I could not have Anagrammatized my Name into some Concealment; or I would have referr'd it to be found in the second Chapter of the second Syntagm of Selden de Diis Syris. Whereas now I freely confess 'tis COTTON MATHER that has written all these things.

Me, me, ad sum qui scripsi; in me convertite Ferrum (MC 107).

KENNETH MURDOCK: "It is I who have written; turn the sword against me" (MC 107).

NOAH WEBSTER: Language, as well as the faculty of speech, was the *immediate gift of God* (WD xxiii).

ANN HUTCHINSON: So to me by an immediate revelation.

DEPUTY GOVERNOR: How! an immediate revelation (AC 337).

ERRATA: We will now, with your Excellency's leave, inquire what *was* the sense of our ancestors (LH 389).

JOHN ADAMS: How vain, and empty is Breath! (JA 45)

JAMES K. HOSMER: When Hutchinson fled from his home on Milton Hill, June 1, 1774, he left his house in charge of his gardener (LH xxiii).

* * *

Appendix

PREDESTINATIONIST (An Immediate Forerunner): Some broken imperfect little clause. Antinomian. She asked.
Extract. Though her eyes could not get out of her mouth. She said.
Interrogator. Opened her mouth in the cold air. "God's compassion towards wise and foolish virgins" (W 2:423). Eloquence eloquence. Flood of confession. But I don't know. Degree. Arminian. Nothing now. Remember that. Is this consistent? I can't believe it.

* * *

CAPTAIN VERE: The heart here, sometimes the feminine in man, is as that piteous woman, and hard though it be, she must here be ruled out (BB 111).

Billy Budd, Sailor (An Inside Narrative), Herman Melville's anachronistic testament or final signal, wasn't published in his lifetime.

"God bless Captain Vere!" (BB 123).

At sea long ago, a conventional felon's syllables of untamed thought are benediction and salute to the commander who could have been his father.

Billy the Handsome-Sailor-Peacemaker-Felon with his welkin-eyed rosebud English complexion could be a virgin foundling. We will never find out. Under the law of the Mutiny Act difference is certain. *Rights-of-Man Bellipotent Atheiste.* The role of Christ is also confused. We call him Authority Love and Faithfulness. We have little assurance. Brute force will beat the weaker part off. Noise for a time then down. 1797. Corroborate. The Court sits silent. Alone but all of Europe.

* * *

Common Sense

Thomas Paine is a marginal figure.

Born 1737. Thetford, England.

Works with father as a corsetmaker. Runs away to sea. Dover. November 1774 arrives in Philadelphia. Radical alternatives. Revolutionary zeal. Federate. The common wants of men essentially *The Rights of Man*, Part 1, dedicated to George Washington.

After the French Revolution a reaction takes place, first in England and then on this side of the Atlantic, during the darkness of which Cheetham slips in his *Life of Paine*.

1792: Outlawed in England.
1802: Goes to New York and lives quietly.
1802: Now a hated figure by Federalists.
1809: Dies in poverty and public disgrace (June 8) in New York City.

BRUCE KUKLICK: Alfred Owen Aldridge's *Thomas Paine's American Ideology* (Dover, Del., 1984) concentrates on Paine's writing as reflecting colonial revolutionary ideals, while A. J. Ayer's *Thomas Paine* (London, 1988) treats Paine's ideas systematically. R. R. Fennesy, *Burke, Paine, and the Rights of Man* (The Hague, 1963) is a comparative study (PW xxii–iii).

THOMAS PAINE: The rational world is my friend, because I am the friend of its happiness (PW 202).

* * *

Criminal Justice

BILLY BUDD: And good-bye to you too, old *Rights-of-Man* (BB 49).

* * *

Common Sense–American Crisis–Rights of Man–Age of Reason

"God bless Captain Vere!"

The time of the archangelic cry is almost dawn.

Morning in emblematical trim. Then Billy ascending. Common plea and common prayer; Baby Budd to the sepulcher of precedents.

Exhort. Spare my life. *Object.* Divorced from the law.

The Lamb of God is slain from the beginning. Reason will trample on a force field of passionate enunciation. The lot falls on Jonah who is sleeping. Quietism is apathy charged with sedition.

What is meant by judgment first.

Imagine His Excellency Thomas Hutchinson Esquire, Governor. His last speech to both Houses: "I see the ways of Providence are mysterious."

Imagine the Honorable Captain Edward Fairfax Starry Vere. His unsettled conviction. The execution of his calling.

In the service of God's mouth.

Sometimes my mouth stops for the written system. Wherever. But I leave that struggling. I have to say something. Foreign wars and the great original problem. Carnal security comes by degrees hum irony. "It is time that nations should be rational" (PW 201). *Ibid.* Vindication. What is the usual lie? Closeted. Primeval Political Writings.

"Oh Lord make us graceful." A canceled irrelevant phrase. *Use.* "Gen.vi.2, 'They saw the daughters of men,' they let their eyes wander, and their hearts lust" (W 2:384).

Horns of the altar dilemma is an anchor.

The oil they pour on Aaron's head runs down his beard and over the skirts of his clothing. By error? Billy stands gazing while the greasy liquid streams across scribbled passages in Genesis. Conscience is God's conviction. Censure He calls theirs. Convicted person it is presumption. Others may see. Conscience commonly lies still.

Hot and total ruin I have signed my name.

Shouting to the waves.

When I sing I stop stammering.

Dialogue between the GHOST of Thomas Paine just arrived from the Elysian Fields; and a ROYAL CRIMINAL in a wood near Philadelphia:

I am glad to see you. I still love liberty and America. I remember a young prodigal whose name I have forgotten. I am here on an important errand.

Asylum.

Despotism, ostentation, property, civil distinction; if a word is a weapon is this the reason? Is this the end of election? Is this the room of the world?

Circled with a fist in the right margin.

You have already made your exit from what must be thought. Error committed through carelessness or haste is a *blunder*. The minister has shifted the blame and condemned your plan. You have nothing to do but begin.

Suspended by a thread from the compass of language.

* * *

Don't speak quick.

Voices are vessels. We can't express them. Oil and grease of the wise. Civil war is necessary in poetic tragedy. Look that your vessel never be left empty. Morning is called morning. This trope is paint.

Lawyers Experts Clergy, tell me the substance of the Son of man.

Baa be simple spirit is thin.

The new testament I will only touch on now. Because it is so difficult to be asleep and among the dead. Mary thought Jesus was the gardener. When Tabitha saw Peter she sat up. Sheep similitude. Yes Billy was a foundling. Hearts are broken I hope to recover. I quote you their own copy which I have here inserted but their oil is spent.

Thrust your note in my side. When will the foolish ones pray?

* * *

Of Christ's Awakening Cry Before His Coming (W 2:409).

The effect of this cry.

It is a shout of discovery. The voice of the cry of the rod. But Jonah has gone down in the sides of the ship and he lies asleep while waves pass over. In sleep all senses are bound up. In deep sleep. We are buried in sleep. Hemlock grows up in our faces. What did we do? Fabricated history where do we go? Thought stark now now. Calmness closes insistently with us. Communion with the universe and infinite emptiness.

"Do you see?" the Bridegroom says.

* * *

Point-no-Point

The minister has unfolded this Parable.

Our lamps are hung up to discover.

What was the wound of these five foolish virgins? They were ready to buy. They had vessels full and lamps burning. But time is irrevocably past as a shadow.

Christ calls his church "my love and my dove."

In the ark or ship we murmur and question.

Assurances, citations, expressions, dams, figments, errors, echolalic slivers, are emblazoned ciphers of Inspiration.

I am pulling representation from the irrational dimension love and knowledge must reach.

Our lamps are out. For what should we watch?

"All adrift to go?" (BB 132).

* * *

THOMAS SHEPARD: Yet we could not go back when we had gone so far. And the Lord saw it good to chastise us for rushing onward too soon and hazarding ourselves in that manner, and I had many fears, and much darkness (I remember) overspread my soul, doubting of our way, yet I say we could not now go back. Only I learnt from that time never to go about a sad business in the dark, unless God's call within as well as that without be very strong and clear and comfortable (GP 57).

BROTHER CRACKBONE HIS WIFE: Yet heard I was under wings of Christ, one of them yet not under both (C 140).

Key

AC *The Antinomian Controversy*: David Hall, ed.
AP *On the Psalms*: St. Augustine.
JA *Adams Papers*, Vol. 2, *Diary*: John Adams.
BB *Billy Budd, Sailor*: Herman Melville; Hayford and Sealts, eds.
C *Confessions*: Thomas Shepard.
CD *The Critical Difference*: Barbara Johnson.
CS *Autobiography of Thomas Shepard*: The Colonial Society of Massachusetts.
GM *A Grammar of Motives*: Kenneth Burke.
GP *God's Plot: The Paradoxes of Puritan Piety, Being the Autobiography & Journal of Thomas Shepard*: Michael McGiffert, ed.
HMB *The History of the Colony and Province of Massachusetts-Bay*: Thomas Hutchinson; Lawrence Shaw Mayo, ed.
L *The Letters of Emily Dickinson*: Johnson and Ward, eds.
LH *The Life of Thomas Hutchinson*: James K. Hosmer.
M *Magnalia Christi Americana*: Cotton Mather.
MB *Manuscript Book*: Thomas Shepard's "T• {*My Birth & Life*} S."
MBED *The Manuscript Books of Emily Dickinson*: R. W. Franklin, ed.
MC *Magnalia Christi Americana*, Books 1 and 2: Kenneth B. Murdock, ed.
ML *The Master Letters of Emily Dickinson*: R. W. Franklin, ed.
OTH *The Ordeal of Thomas Hutchinson*: Bernard Bailyn.
OUD *The Oxford Universal Dictionary*.
PT *The Piazza Tales*: Herman Melville; Hayford, MacDougall, and Tanselle, eds.
PW *Political Writings*: Thomas Paine; Bruce Kuklick, ed.
RR *The Rhetoric of Religion*: Kenneth Burke.
S *The Scapegoat*: René Girard.
TP *A Theory of Literary Production*: Pierre Macherey.
W *The Works of Thomas Shepard*: John A. Albro, ed.
V *Verbal Art, Verbal Sign, Verbal Time*: Roman Jakobson.
WD *An American Dictionary of the English Language*: Noah Webster.
WH *The History of New England from 1630 to 1649*: John Winthrop; James Savage, ed.
WWP *Wonder-Working Providence*: Edward Johnson.
YS *The Yale Gertrude Stein*.

Sources

Adams, John. *Diary and Autobiography of John Adams*. Vol. 2, *Diary 1771–1781*. Edited by L. H. Butterfield. *The Adams Papers*, Series 1. Cambridge, Mass.: The Belknap Press, Harvard University Press, 1961.

Augustine, Saint. *On the Psalms*. 2 vols. Translated and annotated by Hegnin, Dame Scholasta, and Corrigan, Dame Felicitas. Vols. 29 and 30 of *Ancient Christian Writers: The Works of the Fathers in Translation*. London: Longmans, Greene, 1960–61.

Bailyn, Bernard. *The Ordeal of Thomas Hutchinson*. Cambridge, Mass.: The Belknap Press, Harvard University Press, 1974.

Burke, Kenneth. *A Grammar of Motives*. New York: George Braziller, 1955.
———. *The Rhetoric of Religion: Studies in Logology*. Boston: Beacon Press, 1961.
Caldwell, Patricia. *The Puritan Conversion Narrative: The Beginnings of American Expression*. Cambridge and London: Cambridge University Press, 1983.
Dickinson, Emily. *The Letters of Emily Dickinson*. 3 vols. Edited by Thomas H. Johnson and Theodora Ward. Cambridge, Mass.: The Belknap Press, Harvard University Press, 1958.
———. *The Manuscript Books of Emily Dickinson*. 2 vols. Edited by R. W. Franklin, Cambridge, Mass.: The Belknap Press, Harvard University Press, 1981.
———. *The Master Letters of Emily Dickinson*. Edited by R. W. Franklin. Amherst, Mass.: Amherst College Press, 1986.
Girard, René. *The Scapegoat*. Translated by Yvonne Freccero. Baltimore: Johns Hopkins University Press, 1986.
Hall, David D. *The Antinomian Controversy, 1636–1638: A Documentary History*. Edited by David D. Hall. Middletown, Conn.: Wesleyan University Press, 1968.
Hosmer, James K. *The Life of Thomas Hutchinson: Royal Governor of the Province of Massachusetts Bay*. Boston and New York: Houghton Mifflin, 1896.
Hutchinson, Thomas. *The History of the Colony and Province of Massachusetts-Bay*. Edited by Lawrence Shaw Mayo. Cambridge, Mass.: Harvard University Press, 1936.
Jakobson, Roman. *Verbal Art, Verbal Sign, Verbal Time*. Edited by Krystyna Pomorska and Stephen Rudy. Minneapolis: University of Minnesota Press, 1985.
Johnson, Barbara. *The Critical Difference: Essays in the Contemporary Rhetoric of Reading*. Baltimore: Johns Hopkins University Press, 1980.
Johnson, Edward. *Wonder-Working Providence of Sions Savior in New-England*. 1654. Reprint, Delmar, N.Y.: Scholars Facsimile and Reprints, 1974.
Macherey, Pierre. *A Theory of Literary Production*. Translated by Geoffrey Wall. London: Routledge & Kegan Paul, 1978.
Mather, Cotton. *Magnalia Christi Americana: or, The Ecclesiastical History of New-England*. 2 vols. Hartford, Conn.: Silas Andrus & Son, 1855.
———. *Magnalia Christi Americana*, Books 1 and 2. Edited by Kenneth B. Murdock. Cambridge, Mass.: The Belknap Press, Harvard University Press, 1977.
Melville, Herman. *Billy Budd, Sailor (An Inside Narrative)*. Edited by Harrison Hayford and Merton M. Sealts, Jr. Chicago: University of Chicago Press, 1962.
———. *The Piazza Tales, and Other Prose Pieces*. Edited by Harrison Hayford, Alma A. MacDougall, and G. Thomas Tanselle. Evanston and Chicago: Northwestern University Press and the Newberry Library, 1987.
The Oxford Universal Dictionary. London: Amen House, 1933.
Paine, Thomas. *Political Writings*. Edited by Bruce Kuklick. Cambridge: Cambridge University Press, 1989.
Shepard, Thomas. "Autobiography." Edited by Allyn Bailey Forbes. *Publications of the Colonial Society of Massachusetts*, vol. 27 (*Transactions*, 1927–1930).
———. *God's Plot: The Paradoxes of Puritan Piety, Being the Autobiography & Journal of Thomas Shepard*. Edited by Michael McGiffert. Amherst, Mass.: University of Massachusetts Press, 1972.
———. *Manuscript Book*. Unpublished. The Houghton Library, Harvard University, Cambridge, Mass.
———. *Thomas Shepard's "Confessions."* Edited by George Selement and Bruce C. Woolley. In *Collections of the Colonial Society of Massachusetts*, vol. 58. Boston: The Society, 1981.

———. *The Works of Thomas Shepard.* 3 vols. Edited by John A. Albro. 1853. Reprint, New York: AMS, 1967.

Stein, Gertrude. "Patriarchal Poetry." In *The Yale Gertrude Stein*, edited by Richard Kostelanetz. New Haven, Conn.: Yale University Press, 1980.

Webster, Noah. *An American Dictionary of the English Language*. Revised and enlarged by Chauncey A. Goodrich. Springfield, Mass.: George and Charles Merriam, 1852.

Winthrop, John. *The History of New England from 1630 to 1649*. 2 vols. Edited by James Savage. Boston: Phelps and Farnham, 1825.

Quasi-marginalia

In the July 1991 issue of *The William and Mary Quarterly*, "Notes and Documents" section, Mary Rhinelander McCarl, "a certified archivist and librarian," transcribed and reported sixteen more relations of religious experience from a recently discovered notebook Thomas Shepard had used between May 1648 and 1649. McCarl says the notebook had lain unrecognized among the Mather Papers (Box 13, item 7) since 1814, when Isaiah Thomas acquired the collection from Hannah Mather Crocker. Called in to examine the manuscript, McCarl noticed the name of one of the confessors, Daniel Gookin, who was a member of Shepard's Cambridge church. Comparing this volume with Shepard's notebook in the rare book vault at the New England Historic Genealogical Society, she recognized the minister's handwriting.

Isaiah Thomas had labeled the notebook "Memorandum of a minister in Boston or its vicinity 1648. Visits to Criminals etc."

The Captivity and Restoration of Mrs. Mary Rowlandson

I

Náwwatuck nôteshem | *I came from farre.* (K 3)

Come, behold the works of the Lord, what dissolations he has made in the Earth. Of thirty seven persons who were in this one House, none escaped either present death, or a bitter captivity, save only one, who might say as he. *Job* 1.15. *And I only am escaped alone to tell the News.* (N 4)

The Soveraignty & Goodness of GOD, *Together, With the Faithfulness of His Promises Displayed; Being a* NARRATIVE *Of the Captivity and Restauration of Mrs. Mary Rowlandson, Commended by her, to all that desires to know the Lords doings to, and dealings with Her* was probably written in 1677 by a Puritan woman "Especially to her dear Children and Relations" as a reminder of God's Providence. It was printed in Boston in 1682. Avatar of the only literary-mythological form indigenous to North America, this captivity narrative is both a microcosm of colonial imperialist history and a prophecy of our contemporary repudiation of alterity, anonymity, darkness.

Rowlandson's "True History" was enormously popular at once. Her captivity narrative ushered in a host of others. Throughout the eighteenth century, captivity narratives dominated all other North American forms of frontier literature.

Originally, these narratives were simple first-person accounts of a real situation. As time went on and their popularity increased, they were increasingly structured and written down by men, although generally narrated by women.

Protestant sermons came to rely heavily on each captive woman's suffering and deliverance as a metaphor for the process of Conversion.

* * *

> Behold the worthies of *Christ*, as they are boldly leading forth his Troopes into these *Westerne* Fields, marke them well Man by Man as they march, terrible as an Army with Banners, croud in all yee that long to see this glorious sight, see ther's their glorious King *Christ* one that white Horse, whose hoofes like flint cast not only sparkes, but flames of fire in his pathes. Behold his Crown beset with Carbunkles, wherein the names of his whole Army are written. Can there be ever night in his Presence, whose eyes are ten thousand times higher than the Sun? Behold his swiftnes, all you that have said, where is the promise of his comming? (WWP 23–24)

Early New England rhetoric claimed for every single Christian a particular evangelical and secular use and progress. Individual identity was prophetic and corporate. In the hermeneutics of the Bay Colony every member of the Elect was a figural type on the way of federal eschatology. The break with the Old World was a rupture into contraries.

Split forever in the discontinuous drama of Promised Americanus, God is a thunderer, a clockmaker, a deer tamer. There is always a political message in the language of grace. Progress. Watch democratic King-birds and naked Nature.

A harsh climate, a wilderness, tomahawks, powwows, quickhatch and wampumpeag confronted the immigrant children of the Morning.

Bleak necessity caused millenarian affirmations of destiny to thrive on misery. At Boston in New England, the distinguishing mark of a saint was that he or she could transcend adversity. Extremity was every Puritan's opportunity.

> For *Englands* sake they are going from *England* to pray without ceasing for *England*, O *England*! . . . and for this their great enterprise counted as so many crackt-braines, but Christ will make all the earth know the wisdome he hath indued them with, shall over-top all the humane policy in the World, as the sequell wee hope will shew. (WWP 27)

Mary Rowlandson suffered for and was redeemed (ransomed) by her community. Typology projects theocracy into our fictive future.

* * *

While helping the original inhabitants of Earth's millennial fourth corner to become Christians, members of the moral and profit-seeking Elect helped themselves to land. As white settlers increasingly encroached on Native American territory and the precarious food supply was depleted, hostilities became inevitable. In 1645 the white population was estimated at seventeen thousand. Boston was only forty-four years old, but already the city was ringed by rapidly growing villages. Dunstable, Groton, Marlborough, Wrentham, and Lancaster were at the outermost ring from the city center. Beyond Lancaster, trails of the Nipmunk Indians led away into unsettled wilderness.

In 1675, Metacomet (King Philip), the son of Massasoit and chief sachem of the Wampanoags, formed an alliance between his people and the powerful Narragansetts and Nipmunks. These tribes were all part of the loosely connected Algonquian language group. King Philip's War (as it came to be called by the English) rapidly developed into an Algonquian assault on colonists everywhere in New England and was the most serious threat to English interests to date. Contradictory motives, including their own bitter understanding that efforts to bring the Indians to God had miserably failed, soon had the colonists fighting a bitter and bloody race war against the forces of "Diabolism."

> I have read of a great City that was destroyed by Ants; and of another that was destroyed by Rats, and of whole Countreys that have been depopulated by Frogs, yea by Fleas. Though the Indians are a *Despicable* Enemy, yet the Lord is able to cut us down by a small *Indian axe*. But though I thus speak, I believe that God will reform his people by this Judgment, by this shall the Inquiry of Jacob be purged, and this shall be all the fruit to take away his sin. (BH 175–76)

During the difficult years of Indian wars, frequent epidemics, poor harvests, threats from schismatics, and widespread political and financial insecurity, a written emblematic procession of first-generation founding fathers asserted the sacred and corporate success of their pioneering errand-enterprise. First-generation founding mothers generally went unmentioned. Often they died young, worn out by frequent childbearing.

* * *

> It was easie to conjecture that the *Narraganset*, and *Nipmuck* and *Quabaog*, and *River Indians*, being all come together, and the *Army* returned, they would speedily fall upon the *Frontier Towns*. . . . For upon the 10*th* day of *February* some hundreds of the *Indians*

> fell upon Lancaster. . . . Mr. *Rowlandson* (the faithful Pastor of the Church there) had his House, Goods, Books, all burned; his Wife and all his Children led away Captive before the Enemy. Himself (as God would have it) was not at home, whence his own person was delivered, which otherwise (without a Miracle) would have been endangered. Eight men lost their lives, and were stripped naked by the *Indians*, because they ventured their lives to save Mrs. *Rowlandson.* (BH 110–11)

Increase Mather misrepresented the real event: Mrs. Rowlandson was eager and able to save herself. "*I had often before this said, that if the* Indians *should come, I should chuse rather to be killed by them then taken alive* but when it came to the tryal my mind changed" (N 5).

* * *

Mary White Rowlandson, one of the seven children of John and Joane White, was born in England. The date of her birth is uncertain, but the Whites crossed to Salem, Massachusetts, in 1638 and moved to Lancaster in 1653. John White was the wealthiest member and largest landholder of the small frontier settlement. In 1656, Mary married Joseph Rowlandson, the first minister of Lancaster's parish. The couple had four children. Mary, born in 1657, died before she was a year old. Joseph was born in 1662, another Mary in 1665, and Sarah in 1669. Their house was both a dwelling place for the minister and his family and a fortified garrison for the entire community. Through the marriages of her sisters, Mrs. Rowlandson was connected to many other Lancaster land-owning families. Nineteen relatives were in the Rowlandson garrison on the day it was attacked. She said her life had been easy until that morning.

Joseph Rowlandson also was born in England, probably in 1631. His family emigrated to America the same year as the Whites; 1638 was one of the great years of migration. Twenty-three ships and three thousand passengers arrived in the Bay Colony during that year alone. The Rowlandsons settled in Ipswich.

In 1651, Joseph, then beginning his senior year at Harvard College, was sentenced to be fined and publicly whipped for the crime of having written a pasquinade in prose and verse that was posted on the door of the Ipswich Courthouse. Later someone said of the accuser who had charged Rowlandson with libel to himself and others: "when he lived in our country, a wet Eeles tayle and his word were something worth ye taking hold of." But the case was tried in Ipswich by John Endicott, Simon Bradstreet, and William Hathorne. The intimidated and chastened sinner produced a penitent, obedient retraction beginning: "Forasmuch as I Joseph Rowlandson through the suggestion of Satan, and the evil of my owne heart, by that being strongly attemted, by the depravation of this too facilly inclined to the perpetration of a fact whose nature was anomic, and circumstances enormities . . ." (N 155).

Conduct charts are moral thunder in the American creed. Joseph Rowlandson was the only graduate of Harvard's class of 1652.

For the next two years Rowlandson prepared for the ministry, and in 1654 he began preaching in Lancaster. There his mother, father, and brother Thomas soon joined him. He seems to have been well liked by his flock. Twenty years later, when a quarrel arose over the formation of the Old South Church in Boston and the most learned and judicious ministers in Massachusetts were gathered together for advice, he was among the chosen arbiters. When Lancaster was raided and burned and his wife and children carried off, Rowlandson was in or near Boston petitioning colonial officials for troops to guard the village. Lancaster had already been raided once during the previous summer. Later he spent a great deal of time and effort appealing to the Massachusetts Council to arrange for the ransom and release of his family.

Shortly after Mrs. Rowlandson's release, her children also were ransomed. The reunited family lived in and around Boston until 1677, when they moved to Wethersfield, Connecticut, where Joseph Rowlandson had been called as minister. He died at forty-six the following year. Mary Rowlandson's name was listed in the town records of 1679. She had been granted an annual pension of £ 30. It was never paid.

> *He holdeth our soul in life, and suffers not our feet to be moved, for thou our God hast proved us, thou hast tryed us, as silver is tryed.* (N iv, from Psalm 66:9–10)

Historians assumed until recently that because her pension was never collected, Mary died shortly after her husband. In 1985, David Greene, in an article called "New Light on Mary Rowlandson," published in *Early American Literature*, demonstrated that genealogical records of the Talcott family show Mary White Rowlandson married Captain Samuel Talcott on August 6, 1679. Talcott was a prosperous Wethersfield farmer who had been a member of the War Council during King Philip's War. Mary

White Rowlandson Talcott outlived her second husband. When she died at Wethersfield, January 5, 1710, she was in her early seventies.

* * *

2
Communication

Manittóo wússuck-wheke | *God's Booke or Writing* (K 136)

On the tenth of *February* 1675, Came the Indians with great numbers upon *Lancaster*; Their first coming was about Sun-rising; hearing the noise of some Guns, we looked out; several Houses were burning, and the Smoke ascending to Heaven. (N 1)

On this late winter day the vulnerable village of Lancaster in the new Jerusalem of New England feels the sword without and terror within. At sun-rising, on a day of calamity, at the inverted point of antitypical history, Mary Rowlandson looks out at the absence of Authority and sees we are all alone. Spite is the direction of creation. In a minute death can and will come. All collectivities will be scattered to corners.

Epigraph to *The Soveraignty & Goodness of* GOD from the canticle of Moses:

> DEUT. 32.29. *See now that I, even I am he, and there is no God with me: I kill and I make alive, I wound and I heal neither is there any can deliver out of my hand.*

Near the beginning of redemptive time Moses spoke his savage song to the disobedient children of Israel. Now the God who has brought his select nation across an ocean and baptized them in another wilderness has rebuked and ensnared them.

In a sermon delivered at the outbreak of King Philip's War, Increase Mather told his congregation that God decreed their privilege and pattern before the world began. Sanctified affliction must be every saint's portion.

Increase Mather lived safely in Boston.

Mary Rowlandson is a backwoodswoman, and God's hatred stretches farther than his love. Her quiet village is now a site of terror. At this tragic site to what end does the world go on? The Mosaic song is a chant of Combat. The sound is malign.

* * *

In the first paragraph of the first published narrative written by an Anglo-American woman, ostensibly to serve as a reminder of God's Providence, guns fire, houses burn, a father, mother, and sucking child are killed by blows to the head. Two children are carried off alive. Two more adults are clubbed to death. Another escapes—another running along is shot. Indians strip him naked then cut his bowels open. Another, venturing out of his barn, is quickly dispatched. Three others are murdered inside their fortification. The victims are nameless. Specificity is unnecessary in whiplash confrontation. Only monotonous enumeration.

In the first chapter of the first published narrative written by an Anglo-American woman, ostensibly to serve as a reminder of God's Providence, twelve Christians are killed by Indians. The author and her youngest daughter are wounded by bullets. The author's brother-in-law is killed while defending her garrison. The author's nephew has his leg broken and is battered to death. The author's eldest sister, seeing "the infidels haling one way and children another, and some wallowing in their own blood," begs these same infidels to kill her, and they do. Finally, the author's two other children (aged fifteen and ten) are pulled away from her sight.

In the first chapter of the first published narrative written by an Anglo-American woman, ostensibly to serve as a reminder of God's Providence, Native Americans are called "murtherous wretches," "bloody heathen," "hell-hounds," "ravenous bears," "wolves."

"There were twenty-four of us taken alive and carried Captive" (N 5).

This is the hasty beginning of Mary Rowlandson's narrative of her sojourn with the Nipmunks and Narragansetts.

She traveled with them as prisoner and slave for eleven weeks and five days.

"I shall particularly speak of the several Removes we had up and down the Wilderness" (N 5).

Someone is here. Now away she must go. Invisible to her people. Out in a gap in the shadows.

A far cry from Anne Bradstreet's polished pious verse. But the two women were contemporaries, and their husbands were builders of Sion.

This terse, tense book tells of prefigured force and the dooms of life. For a time its author was elided, tribeless, lost.

* * *

> Oh the roaring, and singing and dancing, and yelling of those black creatures in the night, which made the peace a lively resem-

> blance of hell. And as miserable was the wast that was there made, of Horses, Cattle, Sheep, Swine, Calves, Lambs, Roasting Pigs, and Fowl [which they had plundered in the Town] some roasting, some lying and burning, and some boyling to feed our merciless Enemies; who were joyfull enough though we were disconsolate. (N 6)

Pitched into a first night, huddled together at the summit of George Hill, captives from Lancaster look down at their burning village.

They are things, abducted from the structure of experience. Rowlandson wraps herself in separateness for warmth. Tyranny precedes morality. Her little girl was broken in a rift of history.

Somewhere Thoreau says that exaggerated history is poetry.

Now the narrative is divided into chapters called Removes. Each Remove is a forced march away from Western rationalism, deep and deeper into Limitlessness, where all illusion of volition, all individual identity may be transformed—assimilated.

We will read no lovely pictures of the virgin forest; no night fishing, no deer hunting, no wildlife identification, no sunsets, no clouds of pigeons flying. Indian towns are smoky and stinking. It is always either snowing or raining, muddy and dreary. Landscape will never transfix her. The beautiful Connecticut River is just another barrier to get across. Rowlandson's apprehension of nature is an endless ambiguous enclosure.

* * *

Mary Rowlandson has been condemned for her lack of curiosity about the customs of her captors (she was starving, wounded, weary), and her narrative has been blamed for stereotypes of Native Americans as "savages" that later developed in this genre of American fiction. These critics skirt the presence in this same genre of an equally insulting stereotype, that of a white woman as passive cipher in a controlled and circulated idea of Progress at whose zenith rides the hero-hunter (Indian or white) who will always rescue her.

But Rowlandson's presentation of truth severed from Truth is a rude effraction into a familiar American hierarchial discourse of purpose and possession. *The Soveraignty & Goodness of* GOD, *Together, With the Faithfulness of His Promises Displayed*, composed in a bloody fragment of the world, is a relentless origin.

* * *

Substitution

A formal ecclesiastical enclosure—God's promise to the elite—confused and assimilated the chaotic genealogy of this colonial archetype. Oh the metempsychosis!

Poor model-muse cut into the cornerstone of New Jerusalem.

You are a passive victim, captured and threatened by a racial enemy until God's providence (later a human hero) can effect your deliverance. You must shelter the masculine covenant as lost lady and lofty idol. You will water the American venture with your tears. "And my knees trembled under me, *And I was walking thorough the valley of the Shadow of Death*" (N 68).

The truth is what you are worth.

* * *

No copy of the first edition of Mary Rowlandson's *Narrative* is known to exist. All of the editions we have now depend on the text of a "Second Addition Corrected and Amended" printed during the same year as the first. Future distortions, exaggerations, modifications, corrections and emendations may endow a text with meanings it never formed. Probably Rev. Joseph Rowlandson, who had once been publicly whipped and fined for writing a satirical prose poem, helped his wife to choose scriptural parallels and referents that would support and censor her narrative at the same time that they entwined the telling in a becoming Christological corporate pattern.

In a culture chiefly concerned with relationships of power and production, lip service is a tall tale. An old rule.

In 1863, during the darkest days of the Civil War, Emerson delivered a lecture called "The Fortune of the Republic." In it he said:

> . . . the Genius or Destiny of America is no log or sluggard, but a man incessantly advancing, as the shadow on the dial's face, or the heavenly body by whose light it is marked.
>
> The flowering of civilization is the finished man, the man of sense, of grace, of accomplishment, of social power. (CW 537)

A woman is hiking through the Republic's corporate eschatology, carrying her dying daughter Sarah.

She is a mother ensnared in God's plan. She has witnessed the destruction of Lancaster/Sion. She and her children are commodities between two hostile armies. What is their legality? What are they worth?

Other to other we are all functions in a system of War.

* * *

> . . . (by my Master in this writing, must be understood *Quanopin*, who was a *Saggamore*, and married King *Phillips* wives Sister; not that he first took me, but I was sold to him by another *Narrhaganset Indian*, who took me when first I came out of the Garison). . . .
>
> I went to see my daughter *Mary*, who was at this same *Indian Town* at a *Wigwam* not very far off, though we had little liberty or opportunity to see one another other: She was about *ten* years old, & taken from the door at first by a *Praying Ind* & afterward sold for a gun. (N 11–12)

Later, when her captors asked Mrs. Rowlandson to set a price on her own head, she did—£ 50 in goods, mostly guns. Not long after her release her two surviving children also were ransomed.

"As *Solomon* sayes, *Mony answers all things*" (N 70).

Sarah was wounded and worthless to her captors. Only her mother remembers.

> . . . down I sat with the picture of death in my lap. About two houres in the night, my sweet Babe, like a Lambe departed this Life, on *Feb. 18, 1675*. It being about *six yeares*, and *five months* old. It was *nine dayes* from the first wounding, in this miserable condition, without any refreshing of one nature or other, except a little cold water. I cannot but take notice, how at another time I could not bear to be in the room where any dead person was, but now the case is changed; I must and could ly down by my dead Babe, side by side all the night after. I have thought since of the wonderfull goodness of God to me, in preserving me in the use of my reason and senses, in that distressed time, that I did not use wicked and violent means to end my own miserable life. (N 10–11)

God brought Mary Rowlandson into a wood where she lost her children and learned what fear is. Now his trace is peace. She says she has thought of God's goodness since. Like the aboriginals she assures us she hates (at the same time noting their frequent acts of kindness to her), Mrs. Rowlandson attributes causation to spiritual force.

* * *

A Sovereign thinks the sun. Form and force begin with Him. If there is evil in the Universe, it is good and therefore marvelous. Law scans the grammar of liberty and surrender. Catastrophe is a matter of fact. Who can open the door of God's face?

Love is a trajectory across the hollow of history.

Captives have been taken for centuries. Some passing matter made it necessary. They stoop sideways far inland; herds of people reentering the Light. What do they want?

> I was turning the leaves *of my* Bible, and the Lord brought me some Scriptures, which did a little revive me, as that Isai. 55.8. *For my thoughts are not your thoughts, neither are your wayes my ways saith the Lord.* And also that, *Psal.* 37.5 *Commit thy way unto the Lord, trust also in him, and he shal bring it to pass.* About this time they came yelping from *Hadly.* (N 35)

Sarah's burial in unmarked Christianography reduces the rational *Designe of all Theologie* to gibberish. Good sense got lost during the Third Remove. The text of America bypassed her daughter.

"*Come, behold the works of the Lord, what dissolations he has made*" (N 4).

Blessed *shall be* thy basket and thy store (Deut. 28:5).

Cursed *shall be* thy basket and thy store (Deut. 28:17).

Here is the way of contradiction.

* * *

> One of the *Indians* that came from *Medfield* fight, had brought some plunder, came to me, and asked me, if I would have a Bible, he had got one in his Basket, I was glad of it, and asked him, whether he thought the *Indians* would let me read? He answered, yes; so I took the Bible and in that melancholy time, it came into my mind to read first the 28 *Chap. of Deut.* which I did, and when I had read it, my dark heart wrought on this manner, *That there was no mercy for me, that the blessings were gone, and the Curses came in their room, and that I had lost my opportunity.* (N 14)

Memory of anonymous thoughtfulness bites the mind that thought it. "Yes" signifying affirmation and permission, must become "No" at once.

Her first choice from God's Book of Wonderful Mercy is a vengeful chapter from Deuteronomy. "Blessings and curses pronounced." Next she links the curses to her violent self-abhorrence. Each step forward seems mired in the passage for this progress that must always recoil back on herself.

Mary Rowlandson's thoroughly reactionary figuralism requires that she obsessively confirm her orthodoxy to readers at the same time she excavates and subverts her own rhetoric. Positivist systems of psychological protection have disintegrated. Indentities and configurations rupture and shift. Her risky retrospective narrative will be safe only if she asserts the permanence of corporate Soveraignty. Each time an errant perception skids loose, she controls her lapse by vehemently invoking biblical authority. "Not what the Selfe will, but what the Lord will," exhorted Thomas Hooker. Joseph Rowlandson warned, "If God be gone, our Guard is gone."

* * *

"Thus the Lord carried me along from one time to another" (N 38).

In New England in the 1670s, the beaver and deer population had precipitously declined. Furs and skins the Indians had always used for clothing were becoming hard to obtain, and they were increasingly forced to rely on European fabrics. Mary Rowlandson found that the tribes she traveled with were well supplied with dry goods and needles. Apart from the works she did for her master and mistress, she used her knitting and sewing skills to do many odd jobs, for which she was paid. King Philip gave her a shilling when she sewed a shirt for his son. With it she bought a piece of horse flesh. She knit stockings for Wettimore and fixed another pair for a warrior. In return for a piece of beef she made a shirt for a squaw's sannup. For a quart of peas she knit another pair of stockings. Someone asked her to sew a shirt for a papoose in exchange for a "mess of broth, thickened with a meal made from the bark of a Tree."

"Often getting alone: *like a Crane, or a Swallow so did I chatter: I did mourn as a Dove, mine eyes fail with looking upward Oh, Lord I am oppressed undertake for me.* Isa. 38. 14" (N 39).

When she was Quannopin's slave, she liked her master, although she despised his wife, her mistress, Wettimore. None of her captors harmed her. Many shared what little they had with her. Although English soldiers had burned their winter supply of corn and driven them from their towns, she never saw a single Native American die from hunger.

Near the end of her narrative she interrupts the homeward direction of her impending restoration with a list of specific criticisms of colonial policies toward her captors. "Before I go any further, I would take leave to mention . . ."; then she stops her slide into Reason's ruin by pushing her readers back to the imperatives of Wonder-Working Providence. "*Help Lord, or we perish*" (N 59, 63).

* * *

The Copy

John Winthrop kept a journal in three manuscript notebooks. In them he recorded events he considered important from the time he set sail for America on the *Arbella* in 1630 until 1644. The first notebook is untitled. The opening twenty-four manuscript pages make up the author's sea journal, and the rest of the notebook takes up the problems of settlement. Early entries are brief and were probably made on the spot. Political and material changes (Winthrop became governor of the colony in June 1630) altered the author's perception of his role as journalist-historiographer. By 1631 the governor had settled into a more retrospective form of record keeping. The best account of Winthrop's changing purpose is Richard S. Dunn's "John Winthrop Writes His Journal" (*William and Mary Quarterly*, April 1984). Dunn says that after 1632 one of Winthrop's priorities in this account of settlement was to clarify and defend his administration. The first notebook had no title. On the first page of the second notebook the author wrote, "3: vol booke of the Annalls of N: England," and on the following page: "A continuation of the Historye of N: England" (RD 186). After his death the Connecticut Winthrops acquired the volumes. Although early historians of New England—William Hubbard, Cotton Mather, Thomas Prince, Ezra Stiles, Jonathan Trumbull, and Jeremy Belknap—all borrowed them from the Winthrop family for examination, the manuscript books remained untranscribed and unpublished. In the 1780s, when Governor Trumbull and his secretary, John Porter, finally deciphered and copied the first two volumes, the third had disappeared among Thomas Prince's books. Noah Webster, who later became the author of the first *American Dictionary of the English Language*, saw the transcripts and arranged for them to be printed at Hartford in 1790. Webster wrote an introduction and some notes for that edition titled *A Journal Of the Transactions and Occurences in the settlement of Massachusetts and The Other New-England Colonies, from the Year 1630 to 1644: written by John Winthrop, Esq, First Governor of Massachusetts: And now first published from a correct copy of the original Manuscript*. Richard S. Dunn says the Webster edition was filled with misreadings and omissions. Dunn says that Winthrop's handwriting is "notoriously hard to read, the ink is faded, the paper is often stained, worn or torn, and the text is studded with marginalia, insertions, cancellations, and underscorings" (RD 185).

In the spring of 1816 the third volume was discovered in the tower of the Old South Church in Boston. This was now added to the first two notebooks owned by the Massachusetts Historical Society. James Savage, a descendant of Anne Hutchinson, and the librarian of the Society, collated the former manuscripts with the 1790 edition, usually called *Winthrop's Journal*, and found many errors. As well as transcribing the new manuscript, he revised the other two. He also included copious footnotes. The Massachusetts Historical Society, with the backing of the legislature, financed the project, and in 1825–1826 the two-volume edition called *The History of New England from 1630 to 1649, by John Winthrop, Esq. First Governour of the Colony of the Massachusetts Bay, From His Original Manuscripts* was published in Boston. In his Preface, Savage wrote: "Of the title of this work, it may be desirable for the reader to understand, that it is the exact language of the author" (WH 1:v). Savage was a sharp reader of Winthrop's hand, and his annotations were extremely thorough. While taking infinite pains with his own marginal annotations, he seems to have considered Winthrop's marginalia, memoranda, and cancellations to be unworthy of transcription. According to Dunn, the editor altered Winthrop's language. Worst of all, Savage borrowed the original notebooks from the Society in order to work on them in his office. There, on November 10, 1825, the second volume, covering the years of the antinomian controversy and the wars against the Pequots and Narragansetts, was destroyed by fire. Fire and burglary have also done away with the original accounts of Anne Hutchinson's two trials.

James Kendall Hosmer, in his reedited version of Winthrop published by Scribner's in 1902, followed Savage in most respects but recalled the word *journal* to its leading position: *Winthrop's Journal: "History of New England, 1630–1649."* He also deleted many of Savage's marginal annotations, divided the narrative into chapters for each year, and cut some "repulsive" passages, including Anne Hutchinson's monstrous birth and William Hatchett's copulation with a cow.

In his introduction, Hosmer wrote: "The *Winthrop* of 1825–1826 took its place at once in the minds of men as the foundation of Massachusetts history, and the importance of the services of Savage was universally recognized: he became a man of mark, attained to the position of president of the

Massachusetts Historical Society, and devoted himself to the genealogical and antiquarian work into which he had been led through his labors upon Winthrop" (WJ 1:17).

In 1931 the Massachusetts Historical Society decided to publish *The Journal of John Winthrop* (their title) in separate installments among the governor's correspondence and other writings in *The Winthrop Papers*. Only one installment was actually published. A new edition of Winthrop's journal-history, edited by Laetitia Yeandle and Richard S. Dunn, is currently in progress. Dunn says it will draw on the labors of his predecessors. Their edition will be called *The Journal of John Winthrop, 1630–1649*. It will be a compromise, he says.

Meanwhile, although there are now holograph copies of the surviving original manuscripts for scholars to consult, holograph copies cannot be depended upon for accuracy. The Massachusetts Historical Society guards the originals from prying historians and other scholars as if they were guarding the Grail.

The Broad Temper of the Proper Historian

James Kendall Hosmer had a complaint about Savage's footnotes: "As to the annotation . . . the former editor had peculiarities of character making him personally racy and interesting, but impairing the excellence of his commentary. His successor in the presidency of the Massachusetts Historical Society, Mr. Charles Francis Adams, aptly compares him to Dr. Samuel Johnson. Like Johnson, Savage, while most laborious, scrupulously honest, and always resolute and unshrinking, was testy, prejudiced and opinionated; he was prone to measure by small local standards." Hosmer is bothered because sometimes the notes are bulkier than the text. "They are encumbered with genealogies of unimportant people and details as to trivial events and obscure localities. While possessed thus by the spirit of the county antiquary rather than by the broad temper of the proper historian, his hates and loves, equally undiscriminating, are curiously, often amusingly, manifest: he has his *bêtes noires* . . . whom he cannot mention without dealing a stout Johnsonian cuff" (WJ 1:18).

James Hosmer assures his readers that notes to the present edition represent the point of view of "a student of history in a large sense. The Anglo-Saxon race is but one of the races of the world" (WJ 1:19).

"We want historians to confirm our belief that the present rests upon profound intentions and immutable necessities. But the true historical sense confirms our existence among countless lost events, without a landmark or point of reference," says Michel Foucault in "Nietzsche, Genealogy, History" (LCP 155).

"For the little humanity that adorns the earth, a relaxation of essence to the second degree is needed. . . . This weakness is needed. This relaxation of virility without cowardice is needed for the little cruelty our hands repudiate," writes Emmanuel Levinas in the final chapter of *Otherwise than Being or Beyond Essence*, called "Outside" (O 185).

* * *

3
Fecundity

Néechaw. | *She is in Travell* (K 149)

John Winthrop was the governor of the Bay Colony during most of the years between 1629 and 1649, when he died in office. The austere first president of the Commissioners of the United Colonies of New England had four wives. When he was seventeen, he married Mary Forth, who bore him six children, including John Winthrop, Jr. She died in 1615. Later that same year the twenty-seven-year-old widower married Thomasine Cloptin, who died in childbirth in 1616. In 1618, Winthrop married Margaret Tyndal. She followed him to America in 1631, gave birth to eight children, and died in 1647. Several months later the sorrowing fifty-nine-year-old widower and father of seventeen offspring married Mrs. Thomasine Cotymore, a widow. The couple had a son the following year, before Winthrop died, March 26, 1649, at sixty-one.

* * *

On March 27, 1638, John Winthrop wrote in his journal-history:

> The wife of one William Dyer, a milliner in the New Exchange, a very proper and fair woman, and both of them notoriously infected with Mrs Hutchinson's errours, and very censorious and troublesome, (she being of a very proud spirit, and much addicted to revelations,) had been delivered of [a] child some few months before, October 17, and the child buried, (being stillborn,) and viewed of none but Mrs. Hutchinson and the midwife, one Hawkins's wife, a rank familist also; and another woman had a glimpse of it, who, not being able to keep counsel, as the other two did, some rumour began

> to spread, that the child was a monster. One of the elders, hearing of it, asked Mrs. Hutchinson, when she was ready to depart; whereupon she told him how it was, and said she meant to have it chronicled, but excused her concealing of it till then, (by advise, as she said, of Mr. Cotton,) which coming to the governour's knowledge, he called another of the magistrates and that elder, and sent for the midwife and examined her about it. At first she confessed only, that the head was defective and misplaced, but being told that Mrs. Hutchinson had revealed all, and that he intended to have it taken up and viewed, she made this report of it, viz. It was a woman child, stillborn, about two months before the just time, having life a few hours before; it came hiplings till she turned it; it was of ordinary bigness; it had a face, but no head, and the ears stood upon the shoulders and were like an ape's; it had no forehead, but over the eyes four horns, hard and sharp; two of them were above one inch long, the other two shorter; the eyes standing out, and the mouth also; the nose hooked upward; all over the breast and back full of sharp pricks and scales, like a thornback; the navel and all the belly, with the distinction of the sex, were where the back should be, and the back and hips before, where the belly should have been; behind, between the shoulders, it had two mouths, and in each of them a piece of red flesh sticking out; it had arms and legs as other children; but, instead of toes, it had on each foot three claws, like a young fowl, with sharp talons. (WH 1:261–62)

He followed this entry almost immediately with another on the following page:

> Another thing observable was, the discovery of it, which was just when Mrs. Hutchinson was cast out of the church. For Mrs. Dyer going forth with her, a stranger asked, what young woman it was. The others answered, it was the woman which had the monster; which gave the first occasion to some that heard it to speak of it. The midwife [Jane Hawkins], presently after this discovery, went out of this jurisdiction; and indeed it was good for her to be gone, for it was known, that she used to give young women oil of mandrakes and other stuff to cause conception; and she grew into great suspicion to be a witch, for it was credibly reported, that, when she gave any medicines, (for she practised physick,) she would ask the party, if she did believe, she could help her, &c.

> Another observable passage was, that the father of this monster, coming home at this very time, was, the next Lord's day, by an unexpected providence, questioned in the church for divers monstruous errours, as for denying all inherent righteousness, &c. which he maintained, and was for the same admonished. (WH 1:263–64)

Within a few pages he reported the premature birth and death of Anne Hutchinson's "monster," born on the Isle of Aquiday in the Narragansett Bay shortly after her arrival there. When the event was announced in open assembly at Boston, Mr. Cotton said it appeared to be "twenty-seven ||singula frusta vel globulos seminis masculini sine ulla mutatione aut mixtura de femina||* and thereupon gathered, that it might signify her errour in denying inherent righteousness, but that all that was Christ in us, and nothing of ours in our faith, love &c." (WH 1:271).

John Cotton's description failed to satisfy the governor. He demanded a further investigation. Mr. Clarke, a physician and minister of the island, who had been called in to assist the Hutchinsons and examine "the issue," was consulted to clear up any doubts. He conveyed further details about the monster—or mass of possible monstrosities—to the Massachusetts authorities.

> I beheld, first unwashed, (and afterwards in warm water,) several lumps, every one of them greatly confused, and if you consider each of them according to the representation of the whole, they were altogether without form; but if they were considered in respect of the parts of each lump of flesh, then there was a representation of innumerable distinct bodies in the form of a globe, not much unlike the swims of some fish, so confusedly knit together by so many several strings, (which I conceive were the beginnings of veins and nerves,) so that it was impossible either to number the small round pieces in every lump, much less to discern from whence every string did fetch its original, they were so snarled one within another. The small globes I likewise opened, and perceived the matter of them . . .

*Savage claims that "the difference in some particular places, between the correct reading of this edition and the erroneous ones of the former edition, is marked by giving the true word or words in the text between parallel lines before and after, and the word or words of the former edition between similar lines in the margin below" (WH 1:xii). On the following page he substitutes a Latin phrase for an English one. It is therefore here unclear whether the Latin that Savage relegates to the lower margin of the page was in the original manuscript or whether the original was in English because that volume was the one destroyed by fire in his office. The English alternative that Savage inserts into the text reads: "Several lumps of man's seed, without any alteration, or mixture of any thing from the woman."

to be partly wind and partly water. . . . The lumps were twenty-six or twenty-seven, distinct and not joined together; there came no secundine after them; six of them were as great as his fist, and one as great as two fists; the rest each less than another, and the smallest about the bigness . . . of a small Indian bean, and like the pearl in a man's eye. . . . Mr. Cotton, next lecture day, acknowledged his errour, &c. and that he had his information by a letter from her husband, &c." (WH 1:272–73)

On December 6, 1638, John Winthrop wrote in his journal-history:

Dorothy Talbye was hanged at Boston for murdering her own daughter, a child of three years old. She had been a member of the church of Salem, and of good esteem for godliness, &c.; but, falling at difference with her husband, through melancholy or spiritual delusions, she sometimes attempted to kill him, and her children and herself, by refusing meat, saying it was so revealed to her, &c. After much patience, and divers admonitions not prevailing, the church cast her out. Whereupon she grew worse; so as the magistrate caused her to be whipped. Whereupon she was reformed for a time, and carried herself more dutifully to her husband, &c.; but soon after she was so possessed with Satan, that he persuaded her (by his delusions, which she listened to as revelations from God) to break the neck of her own child, that she might free it from further misery. This she confessed upon her apprehension; yet, at her arraignment, she stood mute a good space, till the governour [Winthrop himself] told her she should be pressed to death, and then she confessed the indictment. When she was to receive judgment, she would not uncover her face, nor stand up, but as she was forced, nor give any testimony of her repentance, either then or at her execution. The cloth, which should have covered her face, she plucked off and put between the rope and her neck. She desired to have been beheaded, giving this reason, that it was less painful and less shameful. After a swing or two, she catched at the ladder. Mr. Peter, her late pastor, and Mr. Wilson, went with her to the place of execution, but could do no good with her. Mr. Peter gave an exhortation to the people to take heed of revelations, &c. and of despising the ordinance of excommunication as she had done; for, when it was to have been denounced against her, she turned her back, and would have gone forth, if she had not been stayed by force. (WH 1:279)

Savage's footnote to this passage is worth quoting: "The unfortunate husband, whose life had been attempted by her, was, after her execution, excommunicated 'for much pride and unnaturalness to his wife.' See the letter of Hugh Peter in Hutch. I. 371. The original has been seen by me. Perhaps Peter regretted his treatment of Talby, after his own wife was distracted" (WH 1:279).

On April 13, 1645, John Winthrop wrote in his journal-history:

> Mr. Hopkins, the governour of Hartford upon Connecticut, came to Boston, and brought his wife with him, (a godly young woman, and of special parts,) who was fallen into a sad infirmity, the loss of her understanding and reason, which had been growing upon her divers years, by occasion of her giving herself wholly to reading and writing, and had written many books. Her husband, being very loving and tender of her, was loath to grieve her; but he saw his errour, when it was too late. For if she had attended her household affairs, and such things as belong to women, and not gone out of her way and calling to meddle in such things as are proper for men, whose minds are stronger &c. she had kept her wits, and might have improved them usefully and honorably in the place God had set her. He brought her to Boston, and left her with her brother, one Mr. Yale, a merchant, to try what means might be had here for her. But no help could be had. (WH 2:216–17)

Mrs. Hopkins was Elihu Yale's aunt. Some of the inheritance of this weak-minded woman Winthrop's journal-history certifies as mad helped to found New England's second college. In a footnote, Savage supplies the male Yale genealogy and tells the reader that David Yale, her brother, may have been banished from Massachusetts "by the intolerance of the age."

After her husband's death in England, David Yale became the financial guardian of his sister. Mad, bookish Mrs. Hopkins outlived Governor Hopkins and Governor Winthrop. She died in 1698. "I had intended here to introduced the advice of John Winthrop, jr. on the lady's case, in answer to her husband's application and extracts from two letters of Governour Hopkins in which he mentions it, that were found in Vol. XIX. of the Trumbull MSS. belonging to the Massachusetts Historical Society, but that volume perished, with many other treasures, in the sad conflagration of 10 November last," writes Savage in his footnote to the passage (WH 2:217).

Mrs. Hopkins's books, if they were ever published, are still a blank in American literary history. While Anne Bradstreet gained public acceptance as a writer, her sister, Sarah Dudley Keayne, was less fortunate: "My she Cosin Keane [Sarah] is growne a great preacher" (WP 70).

On March 18, 1646, Benjamin Keayne addressed a letter from London "To the Wor[shipful] my honoured Father Tho: Dudley Esqr: Deb Go[vernou]r of the Matacusetts at his House in Roxburie this present in New England." Thomas Dudley was bookish Anne Bradstreet's father:

> HONOURED SIR, That you, and my selfe, are made sorrie by your Daughters inormous, and continued Crimes, is the greatest Cause of griefe that ever befell mee, and the moare because her obstinate continuance in them, is now to mee by her owne letter made as cartaine, as that I am cartaine, I neaver gave her the least just Cause or occasion to provoake her to them: But most of all it greeves mee, that she has ronne so faste from that highth of error in judgment, to that extremitie of error in practisse, (both which you may plainely see in my other lettre) that shee has not lefte mee any roome or way of reconsiliation: And theirefoare as you desier, I do plainely declare my resolution, never againe to live with her as a Husband: What maintinance your selfe expects I know not. this I know (to my cost, and danger,) shee has unwived her selfe and how shee or you can expect a wives maintinance is to mee a wonder. And lastly the breach not being on my parte I shall take it as an honour to be known by the Neame of Sir Your affectionate Sonne and Sarvant
>
> BEN: KAYEN (WP 144)

This was endorsed by Robert Keayne: "A letter of my sonnes to my Brother Dudlye per mr. Graues. mo. 4: 14: 1647 sent open for me to pervse, and to deliuer or keepe it back as I should thinke meete" (WP 144). Instead of keeping it back, the senior Keayne, founder and first captain of The Ancient and Honorable Artillery in Boston, handed the letter over to Governor Winthrop. It can now be found in volume 5 of the *Winthrop Papers*.

The Records of the First Church in Boston, published by the Colonial Society of Massachusetts, show that on the "24th day of the 8th Moneth 1647"

> Our Sister Mrs. Sarah (sometimes the wife of Mr. Beniamin Keayne but who Devorsed from him) having beene formerly Admonished by

> the Church of her Irregular prophecying in mixt Assemblies, and Refusing ordinarily to heare in the Churches of Christ, and not Answering the Church therein, but falling into odious, lewd, and scandalous uncleane behaviour with one Nicholas Hart an Exommunicate person of Taunton, was by our pastor, in the Name of the Lord Jesus, with the Consent of the Church by their silence, and with the Power of the Lord Jesus, Excommunicated out of the Church. (R 49)

Sarah Dudley Keayne, sister of Anne Bradstreet, lost custody of her daughter and was disinherited by her father. James Savage, in a footnote to another passage in the *History* concerning Robert Keayne, supplies copious information about his complicated business practices, fines levied against him, a land grant, and his "endless testament": "Between his only son, Benjamin, and a daughter of Dudley, 'an unhappy and uncomfortable match' is spoken of in this will; and that union, perhaps, with other disagreeable circumstances, compelled the son to return to the land of his fathers, where he died, I presume, in 1668. . . . The male line ended with Benjamin" (WH 1:314–15).

Later, Sarah Keayne married Thomas Pacey, a man from the lower classes. Her subsequent history seems to be blank.

* * *

Anna Bradestreate.
Deer Neat *An Bartas.*

Anne Bradstreate.
Artes bred neat *An.*
(AB 531)

Anne Dudley Bradstreet, Sarah's older sister, a female member of the "Governor and Company of the Massachusetts Bay in New-England," sailed from England to Salem, Massachusetts, with her husband and other Dudley family members on the *Arbella* in March 1630. In *An American Triptych: Anne Bradstreet, Emily Dickinson, Adrienne Rich*, Wendy Martin, whose work on Bradstreet contributes to a deeper understanding of contradictions in her work, falls somewhat short when she describes the poet's father as "a thoughtful and well-informed man who taught his daughter Greek, Latin, French, and Hebrew and encouraged her to read and write poetry" and tells us "she was educated in the Elizabethan tradition that valued female intelligence" (AT 21). Thomas Dudley, one of the most opportunistic and brutal of gentlemen of the first rank in the Bay Colony, was anything but thoughtful at the civil trial of Anne Hutchinson. There he accused her of "venting" her "strange opinions." He said she had "depraved all the ministers" since her arrival in the Bay Colony, and was the "cause of what is fallen out, why we must take away the foundation and the building will fall" (AC 318). Even Cotton Mather remarks in *Magnalia* that Dudley's "*justice* was a perpetual terror to evil-doers." Mather points out and Martin takes note of the fact that poetry was one of Dudley's accomplishments. The patiently meticulous James Savage, in his footnotes to an early passage in Winthrop's journal, supplies a telling epitaph by Governor Belcher:

> Here lies Thomas Dudley, that trusty old stud,
> A bargain's a bargain, and must be made good.
>
> (WH 1:51)

When Bradstreet's father died at seventy-five, July 31, 1653, in Roxbury, Massachusetts, one of his poems was found in his pocket. The last lines read: "Let men of God in courts and churches watch / O'er such as do a *toleration* hatch, / Lest that ill egg bring forth a cockatrice, / To poison all with heresie and vice. / If men be left, and otherwise combine, / My *Epitaph's* I DY'D NO LIBERTINE" (M 1:134).

* * *

> THE | TENTH MUSE | Lately sprung up in AMERICA. | OR | Severall Poems, compiled | with great variety of Wit | and Learning, full of delight. | Wherein especially is contained a com- | pleat discourse and description of | The Four *Elements*, | *Constitutions*, | *Ages of Man*, | *Seasons of the Year*. | Together with an Exact Epitome of | The Four Monarchies, *viz*. | The *Assyrian*, | *Persian*, | *Grecian*, | *Roman*. | Also a Dialogue between Old *England* and | New, concerning the late troubles. | With divers other pleasant and serious Poems. | By a Gentlewoman in those parts. (AB xl)

Anne Bradstreet's first volume of poetry was published in 1650 in London. The book had been set in type, apparently without the author's consent, from a manuscript her minister brother-in-law, John Woodbridge, carried to England in 1647.

Woodbridge's introduction to the first edition assures the "Kind Reader":

> It is the Work of a Woman, honoured, and esteemed where she lives, for her gracious demeanour, her eminent parts, her pious conversation, her courteous disposition, her exact diligence in her place, and discreet mannaging of her family occasions; and more then so, these Poems are the fruit but of some few houres, curtailed from her sleep, and other refreshments . . . and contrary to her expectation I have presumed to bring to publick view what she resolved should never in such a manner see the Sun; but I found that divers had gotten some scattered papers, affected them wel, were likely to have sent forth broken peices to the Authors prejudice. (AB 526)

The first poem in the collection is an abject dedication to Bradstreet's "most Honoured Father, *Thomas Dudley* Esq."

> I shall not need my innocence to clear,
> These ragged lines, will do't, when they appear.
> On what they are, your mild aspect I crave,
> Accept my best, my worst vouchsafe a grave.
>
> From her, that to your selfe more duty owes,
> Then waters, in the boundlesse Ocean flowes.
>
> ANNE BRADSTREET (AB 6)

Between "The four Seasons of the Yeare" and "The Foure Monarchies," the author, or her minister-editor-brother-in-law, inserted another signed filial apology:

> *My Subjects bare, my Brains are bad.*
> *Or better Lines you should have had.*
> *The first fell in so naturally,*
> *I could not tell how to passe't by:*
> *The last, though bad, I could not mend.*
> *Accept therefore of what is penn'd,*
> *And all the faults which you shall spy,*
> *Shall at your feet for pardon cry.*
>
> Your dutifull Daughter.
> *A. B.* (AB 53)

For a woman to break Puritan sanctions against public statements from her sex was revolution enough in seventeenth-century North America.

The madness of Anne Hopkins; the excommunication and banishment of Anne Hutchinson; the banishment of Mary Dyer; published reports of their "monster" premature babies; the reprimands or silencing of other women who were midwives, had medical knowledge, or trangressed the male boundaries of theology by preaching; the excommunication, divorce, and disinheritance of her undutiful sister were ominous precedents. Anne Bradstreet was the daughter of a governor of Massachusetts and the wife of a leading magistrate, both of whom were virulent persecutors of Anne Hutchinson. Yet she seems to have persisted in her determination to keep on reading and writing by carefully controlling the tone of her rebellion.

We can know little about her authorial intentions because original manuscripts for the *Tenth Muse* and almost everything else she wrote have been lost. The surviving copy-texts wear a mask of civility, domesticity, and perfect submission to contemporary dogmatism.

Sometimes Anne Bradstreet's cover slips and a voice of anger breaks out. In her elegy titled "In honour of that High and Mighty Princess, Queen ELIZABETH, of most happy memory," Bradstreet sharply rebuked the slander, consecrated by Saint Paul and emphasized by Anglicans and Puritans, that man was intellectually preeminent over woman.

> Now say, have women worth, or have they none?
> Or had they some, but with our Queen is't gone?
> Nay Masculines, you have thus tax'd us long,
> But she though dead, will vindicate our wrong.
> Let such, as say our sex is void of reason.
> Know 'tis a slander now, but once was treason.
>
> (AB 157)

The lapse was covered by John Woodbridge's ministering nonauthorial hand. In one of the initialed or unsigned commendatory poems and anagrams attesting to her character and literary achievement appended to the first edition, he wrote: "You have acutely in *Eliza*'s ditty / Acquitted women, else I might with pitty. / Have wisht them all to womens Works to look. / And never more to meddle with their book" (AB 528).

Mrs. Bradstreet was usually more discreet.

The Author to her Book.

> Thou ill-form'd offspring of my feeble brain.
> Who after birth did'st by my side remain.
> Till snatcht from thence by friends, less wise then true
> Who thee abroad, expos'd to publick view.

Made thee in raggs, halting to th' press to trudge,
Where errors were not lessened (all may judg).
At thy return my blushing was not small,
My rambling brat (in print) should mother call,
I cast thee by as one unfit for light,
Thy Visage was so irksome in my sight,
Yet being mine own, at length affection would
Thy blemishes amend, if so I could:
I wash'd thy face, but more defects I saw.
And rubbing off a spot, still made a flaw.
I stretcht thy joynts to make thee even feet,
Yet still thou run'st more hobling then is meet:
In better dress to trim thee was my mind.
But nought save home-spun Cloth, i' th' house I find.
In this array, 'mongst Vulgars mayst thou roam,
In Criticks hands, beware thou dost not come:
And take thy way where yet thou art not known.
If for thy Father askt, say, thou hadst none:
And for thy Mother, she alas is poor.
Which caus'd her thus to send thee out of door.

(AB 177–78)

"The Author to her Book" was added to the Bradstreet canon in the posthumous 1678 edition called *Several Poems*, "Corrected by the Author, and enlarged," along with seventeen other previously unpublished works apparently found among her papers after her death. Joel R. McElrath, Jr., and Allan J. Robb, the editors of the *The Complete Works of Anne Bradstreet*, published in 1981, call this poem one of her "truly charming" works.

* * *

To the READER.

Good READER,

As large Gates to small Edifices, so are long Prefaces to little Bookes, therefore I will breifly informe thee, that here thou shalt find, the time when, *the manner* how, *the cause* why, *and the great successe* which *it hath pleased the Lord to give, to this handfull of his praysing saints in* N. Engl. *and it will be clearely demonstrated, if thou compare them, with any other people, who have left their Countryes, as the* Gothes, Vandals &c. *to possesse a fatter, as* Italy, *or warmer,* as Spaine, &c. (WWP A2)

Edward Johnson, a woodworker who may at one time have been a shipbuilder, also arrived in Salem in 1630, probably on the *Arbella*. This time he came alone. He was back in England between 1631 and 1635. In 1636 he returned to Boston with his wife and children. Eventually, Johnson became one of the founders of Woburn, the town's first "Recorder," a trader, a captain in the militia and surveyor-general of arms and munitions for the colony. In 1654, Johnson was the anonymous author of the first published history of Massachusetts, *Wonder-Working Providence of Sion's Savior in New-England*. This history lavished praises on Anne Bradstreet's illustrious father, Governor Thomas Dudley, and on her husband, Simon: "*Now* Simon *yong, step in among, these worthies take thy place: / All day to toile in vinyard, while Christ thee upholds with grace*" (WWP 108). Simon later became governor.

* * *

Anne Hutchenson

a non-such (M 2:517)

"And verily Satans policy here . . . was to keepe men from that one right way . . . no marvell then if so many Errours arise, like those fained heads of *Hidra* as fast as one is cut off two stand up in the roome, and chiefly about the uniting of the Soule to Christ by Faith" (WWP 93).

Captain Johnson excoriated Anne Hutchinson in chapter after chapter. She is the Hydra in his Song of America.

> Come along with me sayes one of them [Erronists], i'le bring you to a Woman that Preaches better Gospell then any of your black-coates that have been at the Ninneversity, a Woman of another kinde of spirit, who hath had many Revelations of things to come, and for my part, saith hee, I had rather hear such a one that speakes from the meere motion of the spirit, without any study at all, then any of your learned Scollers, although they may be fuller of Scripture (I) and admit they may speake by the helpe of the spirit, yet the other goes beyond them . . . the grosse dissimulation of these erronious persons hath appeared exceedingly, as for instance first of a Woman, even the grand Mistris of all the rest, who denied the Resurrection from the dead, shee and her consorts mightily rayling against learning, perswading all they could to take heed of being spoyled by it . . . so that surely had this Sect gone on awhile, they would have made a new Bible. (WWP 95–97)

Epigraph to *A History of New-England, From the English planting in the Yeere 1628, untill the Yeere 1652,* declaring the form of their Government, from the Book of Psalms:

> 107.24 *The righteous shall see it and rejoice, and all iniquity shall stop her mouth* (WWP A1).

* * *

After the death of her husband in Rhode Island in 1642, the banished "nimble-tongued woman" and ten of her children moved to Long Island Sound near what is present-day Rye, in Westchester County, New York. Like many other fugitives from the Bay Colony's theocracy, the Hutchinsons moved farther away into uncharted areas to avoid official harassment. When they decided on the Dutch settlements near New Amsterdam, they were probably unaware of the brutal attacks Dutch colonists had made on the Siwanoy Indians during 1643. Anne Hutchinson had experienced friendly relations with the natives of Rhode Island. As Johnson scornfully put it in his history, "being amongst a multitude of Indians, [they] boasted they were become all one Indian" (WWP 132). A few months after her arrival, John Throckmorton, another dissenter from New England, settled nearby. In August or September, just after the harvest, both settlements were attacked and destroyed as part of a larger Mohegan uprising. Anne Hutchinson and most of her company were killed. Their house was burned beyond trace.

* * *

Edward Johnson, the soon-to-be captain-adventurer-trader and anonymous historian-narrator of *Wonder-Working Providence of Sions Savior in New-England*, arrived for the second time in the Massachusetts Bay Colony, in 1636, at the height of the antinomian controversy.

Vulnerability and Contact

"Here I am."

Mattacusets These in new England:

"Then my deare friend unfold thy hands, for thou and I have much worke to doe. I and all Christian Souldiers" (WWP 26).

"Now, now: I now in hand for the exalting of his glorious Kingdome" (WWP 117). Strangers make signs in a babbling. There is buzzing. Books called *Appeals to the People*. I am no tolerator. Substitution is not an act. Reassemble the subject in bearing it.

Election. Application of the law or precedent. This is the state. Definitive sentence. Immanent. Engender the sense of the term. Passivity is negligent maternity. Not to shut up in it.

These theses drive off skepticism. This ladder-proof account is itself. Errors of which you will further hear: Eros and separation. A woman should love with her children. To them it is not given. Do to them 1 Kings 21.

The author ends Yours to command.

> Certaine Indians coming to her house, discoursing with them, they wished to tye up her doggs, for they much bit the man, not mistrusting the Indians guile, did so, the which no sooner done, but they cruelly murthered her, taking one of their daughters away with them, & another of them seeking to escape is caught, as she was getting over a hedge, and they drew her back againe by the haire of the head to the stump of a tree, and there cut off her head with a hatchet: the other that dwelt by them betook them to boat, and fled, to tell the sad newes; the rest of their companions, who were rather hardened in their sinfull way, and blasphemous opinions, than brought to any sight of their damnable Errours, as you shall after hear; yet was not this the first loud speaking hand of God against them; but before this the Lord had poynted directly to their [Erronists'] sinne by a very fearfull Monster, that another of these women brought forth they striving to bury it in oblivion, but the Lord brought it to light, setting forth the view of their monstrous Errors in this prodigious birth. (WWP 133)

Between 1651 and 1659, when Captain Johnson was probably writing the twelfth chapter of his history, he combined an earthquake that "came from the Westerne and uninhabited parts of this Wildernesse"; Mrs. Hutchinson's preaching, civil censure, banishment, and murder; and the miscarriage of her supporter and fellow midwife, Mary Dyer, and grouped these signs of creation and conflict with the "timely death of Mr. John Harvard" who left enough money to pay for the erection of New England's first college.

> This yeare, although the estates of these pilgrim people were much wasted, yet seeing the benefit that would accrew to the Churches of Christ and Civil Government, by the Lords blessing, upon learning, they began to erect a Colledge, the Lord by his provident hand giving

his approbation to the work, in sending over a faithfull and godly servant of his, the reverend Mr. *John Harverd*. (WWP 133)

For richest Jems and gainfull things most Merchants wisely venter: / Deride not then New England men, *this Corporation enter*" (WWP 14).

Proximity is fraternity in *Wonder-Working Providence of Sions Savior in New-England*: then who is what to me?

Nettles and brambles feminine.

Colledge is a site of constraint. The system holds together.

* * *

Of the great Earthquake in New England, *and of the wofull end of some erronious persons, with the first foundation of* Harverd *Colledge*. (WWP 131)

God stamps dominion. Good Reader,
learn your letters.
At the margins of the history of the West.

"*If* Harverd *had with riches here been taken. / He need not then through troublous Seas have past*" (WWP 133).

The perils of colonial infancy: Captain Johnson's custom of dropping into poetry. John Winthrop's journal entering into history.

"The fifth volume of the *Winthrop Papers*, covering the years 1645–1649, marks the end of the first chapter of the history of the Winthrop family in America," writes its editor, Allyn B. Forbes (WP v). The *Winthrop Papers* is published by the Massachusetts Historical Society. The frontispiece is a portrait of Governor Winthrop now owned by the American Antiquarian Society in Worcester. This portrait may be only a copy, although portions below the head may be original work. Some say the face was painted by Van Dyke before Winthrop left England. Forbes cites Mr. Burroughs, an authority on something from somewhere. Mr. Burroughs supports the originality of the face due to the "freedom and emphasis" of the brush strokes.

The portrait's donor, William Winthrop, was "the Son of John, the Son of Adam, the Son of Adam, the Son of Adam, the Son of John, Governor of Massachusetts" (WP v).

Can the subject escape the concept? John Harvard was a minister: John Harvard, the son of a butcher.

* * *

In the Trace of Exile

1638: (2.)] The governour, with advice of some other of the magistrates and of the elders of Boston, caused the said monster to be taken up, and though it were much corrupted, yet most of these things were to be seen, as the horns and claws, the scales &c. When it died in the mother's body, (which was about two hours before the birth,) the bed whereon the mother lay did shake, and withal there was such a noisome savour, as most of the women were taken with extreme vomiting and purging, so as they were forced to depart; and others of them their children were taken with convulsions (which they never had before nor after,) and so were sent for home, so as by these occasions it came to be concelaed. (WH 1:263)

1638: (3.) 2.] At the court of elections, the former governour, John Winthrop, was chosen again. . . . This court the name of Newtown was altered, and it was called Cambridge. (WH 1:265)

James Savage's footnote to the latter entry reads:

In compliment to the place, where so many of the civil and clerical fathers of New England had received their education, this venerable name (may it ever be preserved!) was undoubtedly bestowed. There were probably, at that time, forty or fifty sons of the University of Cambridge in Old England—one for every two villages of Massachusetts and Connecticut. The sons of Oxford were not few. (WH 1:265)

Relation to Something

The caress of love. One has just been born. A monist conception. It is a daughter a monster the other. What verb can deliver consolation? Go spend your salt plan. Calculation hear me in your name. What is most uncovered? Bury in water and mud. Never enough. Surrender tender face thou I will not be consoled. 49 Isaiah 21 give place to obscurity that I may show.

A little child scrambles out and comes to its mother.

Genesis Exodus Leviticus Kings Chronicles Judges escaping the birth am rereading chapters. Chapter for child per child.

Awake, awake Deborah; remembering Nebuchadnezzar.

Remembering Nebuchadnezzar go heap coals of fire on chapter.

Interiority of wanton femininity here is the explication I Timothy 12 and the others

Paul to Timothy by the commandment of God:
which is our hope? where are we now?

speck of letter in a sea of silt

Mr. Mather Mr. Hubbard Mr. Prince. Listen to me.

What is finite freedom? Is every founder confounded by error? How is the hammer of the whole earth cut? I hope I will not be unwilling. Always desire to subscribe myself Yours in what I say

Door on the hinge and wheel on the pin I hang and spin and turn again.

Negligence of passivity Love is the interdiction of a history.

* * *

In May 1646, John Winthrop noted in his journal-history:

> A daughter of Mrs. Hutchinson was carried away by the Indians near the Dutch, when her mother and others were killed by them: and upon the peace concluded between the Dutch and the same Indians, she was returned to the Dutch governour, who restored her to her friends here. She was about eight years old, when she was taken, and continued with them about four years, and she had forgot her own language, and all her friends, and was loath to have come from the Indians. (WH 2:267)

James Savage, usually so prolific with his footnotes, has no footnote here.

* * *

Savage History Genealogy

A meticulous gentleman with the surname Savage is transcribing and editing the *History of New England from 1630 to 1649*, written by a founding gentlemen father.

His marginal notes to the passages in Winthrop's *History* concerning Dyer's monster, the monster's witch-midwife, and the questioning in church of the monster's father "for divers monstruous errours" tell us Dyer's future:

> After long enjoying her revelations, in quiet, at Rhode Island, she was unhappily led . . . again to visit Boston, probably bringing more light, when she was condemned to death as a Quaker. Winthrop, governour of Connecticut, our author's eldest son, inheriting the natural mildness of his father, attempted to save her life; but the bigotry of the age had acquired a severer character, and, for a second return, in June, 1660, she suffered. See Hutchinson, I. 184. (WH 1:261*n*)

The title page of *The History of New England from 1630 to 1649, by John Winthrop, Esq. First Governour of the Colony of the Massachusetts Bay, From His Original Manuscripts, With Notes to Illustrate the Civil and Ecclesiastical Concerns, the Geography, Settlement and Institutions of the Country, and the Lives and Manners of the Principal Planters* assures us that James Savage is a member of the Massachusetts Historical Society. Often the edifying margins of this early Victorian American edition overprint the tumultuous record of law in early seventeenth-century Massachusetts Bay Colony. The Massachusetts Historical Society is an organization of men who are elite.

On June 1, 1660, Mary Dyer was hanged with two other Quakers on Boston Common.

"She suffered. See Hutchinson, I 184."

Savage says look somewhere else.

Later Savage becomes a genealogist.

During the 1660s, Commissioner Humphrey Atherton was the chief military officer in New England. While he was the governor of Connecticut, John Winthrop, Jr., became a partner in the Atherton Company. Led by Atherton, the company consisted of a group of land speculators whose double dealings with the Narragansetts made them into wealthy landowners. Rufus Jones, in *The Quakers in the American Colonies*, says that while Mary Dyer's body was swinging in the wind, Humphrey Atherton, who was a witness to the execution, pointed to it and scornfully remarked: "She hangs there as a flag" (QC 89).

Savage's copious footnotes on Humphrey Atherton ("Humphrey Atherton deserves much honor in our early annals") don't cover this incident (WH 2:137).

In the last chapter, called "Friday" of *A Week on the Concord and Merrimack Rivers*, first published in Boston in 1867, Thoreau asks: "But where is the instructed teacher? Where are the *normal* schools?"

* * *

Publish in the margin call attention to something.

Letter to the Massachusetts General Court, March 28, 1659:

> When I heard your last Order read
> it was a disturbance unto me that was
> So freely Offering up my life to him who gave it me
> That was so freely
> Obedience being Presence and Peace and Love in me
> I was so far
> than that.
> Any more the words I should not return to Prison
> I submitted, finding nothing from the Lord to the contrary
> That I may know
> For he is my Life and the length of my Days
> I rested I
> came at his Command and go at his Command
>
> "Mary Dyer" (MD 92–93)

Who were pledged to loyalty? Unevenness in their course. The violence of ambiguity. Disorder is another order. Now it is *qunnantacaun* that is lamentation

my question is: where do we define the
jurisdiction?

Dear sister, I can go no further; a weary body and sleepy eyes command.

Write to the authorities. Not to be known when I sink down. I have made your face wrong. Vulnerable as mortal. In the no man's land I remain Yours forever.

History certifies this.

* * *

4
Outside

Npakénaqun. | *I am put away.* (K 150)

. . . and as for beauty they esteeme black beyond any colour. Wherefore their *Squawes* use that sinful art of painting their Faces in the hollows of their Eyes and Nose, with a shining black, out of which their tip of their Nose appeares very deformed, and their cheeke bone, being of a lighter swart black, on which they have a blew crosse dyed very deepe.

This is the beauty esteemed by them. (WWP 115–16)

For eleven weeks and five days Mary Rowlandson was that "woman in the Wilderness who may have the vomit of the Dragon cast in her face." She saw and spoke to King Philip—the Devil. She was the colonist Sion the outcast.

Returned from daily walking to and fro at the ends of the earth—with Satan—Rev. Joseph Rowlandson's wife knew that her ordeal might mark her as suspect; vulnerable to ambivalent charges ranging from pride (she had set a high price on her own head) to sexual promiscuity, even to sorcery. Perhaps she told her story to assure herself and her community that she was a woman who feared God and eschewed evil.

One precaution first—rupture erased in a cloud of his Glory in the dust of her text.

> *I have been in the midst of those roaring Lyons, and Salvage Bears that feared neither God, nor Man, nor the Devil, by night and day, alone and in company: sleeping all sorts together, and yet not one of them ever offered me the least abuse of unchastity to me, in word or action.* Though some are ready to say, I speak it for my own credit; *But I speak it in the presence of God, and to his Glory.* (N 64)

But her "song of war" tarnishes Captain Edward Johnson's version of the Common-wealth as a figural "refuge" set apart for the encouragement, "cheerfulnesse" and "primitive purity" of these "forerunners of Christs Army."

* * *

Mat pitch cowahick | *The God that made*
Manit keesiteonckqus | *you will not know you.* (K 192)

> Oh yes! oh yes! oh yes! *All you the people of Christ that are here Oppressed, Imprisoned and scurrilously derided, gather yourselves together, your Wives and little ones, and answer to your severall Names as you shall be shipped for his service, in the Westerne World.* (WWP 2)

One of the wives attending to the service of the King of Kings answers to the name of Mary. Mary reapprehends her own story while trapped in

New England's use and progress. Sometimes her husband, Joseph, a godly minister of Christ, is left behind in their Westerne Garden.

Away with her by hidden paths into an origin.

> There were many hundreds, old and young, some sick, and some lame many had *Papooses* at their backs, the greatest number at this time with us, were *Squaws*, and they travelled with all they had, bag and baggage, and yet they got over this River . . . and on *Munday* they set their *Wigwams* on fire, and away they went: On that very day came the *English* Army after them to this River, and saw the smoak of their *Wigwams*, and yet this River put a stop to them. (N 19)

Here is an amorphous psychic space. Only her retrospective narrative voice can control and connect the twists and turns of time past. "*For a smal moment have I forsaken thee, but with great mercies will I gather thee*" (N 38).

Who has forsaken who? Where are we now? God's text in Rowlandson's text is counterpoint, shelter, threat.

"My Bible: *Which was my Guid by day and my Pillow by night*" (N 38).

Soteriology is a screen against the primal Night. She must come back to that knowing.

But in writing Language advances into remembering that there is no answer imagining Desire. Remembering a wild place there is no forgetting.

"Now must we pack up and be gone from this Thicket. . . . As we went along they killed a *Deer*, with a young one in her, they gave me a piece of the *Fawn*, and it was so young and tender, that one might eat the bones as well as the flesh, and yet I thought it very good" (N 41).

Once Mary Rowlandson was quarry to huntsmen. First she hated them then she joined them now she remembers to hate them again.

She and her children with some nieces, nephews, and neighbors crossed into absence on February 10, 1675. Out of sight? What of that?

This is a crime story.

Remember, captives and captors are walking together beyond the protective reduplication of Western culture through another epoch far off. God sent affliction to Lancaster to try her. Witnesses are all humans linking or heralding truth or transgression in a grammatical irruption of grace abounding.

"The *Indians* were as thick as the trees: it seemd as if there had been a thousand Hatchets going at once" (N 20). "*The* Squaw *laid a skin for me, and bid me sit down, and gave me some Ground-nuts, and bade me come again: and told me they would buy me, if they were able, and yet these were strangers to me that I never saw before*" (N 29). "There was here one *Mary Thurston* of *Medfield*, who seeing how it was with me, lent me a Hat to wear" (N 26). "*We took up our packs and along we went. . . .* As we went along I saw an *English-man* stripped naked, and lying dead upon the ground, but knew not who it was" (N 45). "They came home on a Sabbath day, and the *Powaw* that kneeled upon the *Deer-skin* came home (I may say, without abuse) as black as the Devil" (N 52). "*Then came* Tom *and* Peter, *with the second Letter from the Council, about the Captives.* Though they were *Indians*, I gat them by the hand, and burst out into tears" (N 48–49). "There was another Praying *Indian*, so wicked and cruel, as to wear a string about his neck, strung with *Christians* fingers" (N 50). "There was one that kneeled upon a *Deer-skin*, with the company round him in a ring who kneeled, and striking upon the ground with their hands and with sticks; and muttering or humming with their mouths, besides him who kneeled in the ring, there also stood one with a Gun in his hand" (N 51).

* * *

This is a crime story in a large and violent place. Too large for subject and object. Only a few of her captors have names. Nearly all of their names are wrong. Anyway, by 1676 most of them are gone.

1677: "*I can remember the time, when I used to sleep quietly without workings in my thoughts, whole nights together, but now it is other wayes with me.* When all are fast about me, and no eye open, but his who ever waketh, my thoughts are upon things past" (N 71).

Carried away unwillingly into the uncharted geography of North America, an author cannot let some definitive version of New England's destiny pull her. Once she senses oscillations of sense close to the face of her hunger, Scripture is a closure. Allegory a grid she can get over.

When Mary Rowlandson can't count sheep she lets counter-memory out.

Clamor in the theater of alienation. Ransom stammers fact of Famine. Divine cruelty and social necessity unleash the dialectical tension between Starvation and Gluttony.

A narrator is narrating something about the recalcitrant beast in Everywoman. In this wild place every human has a bait she must bite.

> There came an Indian to them at that time, with a basket of Horse-liver. I asked him to give me a piece: *What*, sayes he *can you eat*

> *Horse-liver*? I told him, I would try, if he would give a piece, which, he did, and I laid it on the coals to rost, but before it was half ready they got half of it away from me, so that I was fain to take the rest and eat it as it was, with the blood about my mouth, and yet a savoury bit it was to me: *For to the hungry Soul every bitter thing is sweet.* (N 21–22)

There she stands, blood about her mouth, savoring the taste of raw horse liver. God's seal of ratification spills from her lips or from her husband's pen.

* * *

"There may be two things spoken to in the management of the Truth" (N 134), wrote Rev. Joseph Rowlandson in his "Last Sermon," preached at Wethersfield, November 21, 1676, on a day of FAST and HUMILIATION. This is the sermon annexed to most editions of his wife's narrative of her captivity and restoration. A year later he was dead.

The idiosyncratic syntax of Mary Rowlandson's closed structure refuses closure. After the war-whoop terror and the death of her little daughter, a new management of the truth speaks to oppose itself. When the teller skids into schism remembering, she calls on God to keep her ground from shifting. She is a servant of the Lord. Fidelity is her privilege. Faith is a first precaution. Muttering or humming.

> —Must rely on God himself—whole dependence must be upon him—Guns guns—tobacco—he on the *Deer-skin*—preparation for a great day of Dancing—Bracelets—handfulls of Neck-laces—Garters hung round with Shillings—*God show'd his power over the Heathen in this—there is no thing too hard for God!*
>
> —nothing to drink but water and green Hurtle-berries—
>
> —nothing over them but the heavens, and nothing under them but the earth—
>
> Quonopen fetched me some water himself, and bid me wash, and gave me a Glas to see how I looked. I was wonderfully revived by this favor he showed me—*But to return to my going home—Our family now being gathered together—*

RHYTHM OF THE OLD WORLD: "Here you have Samson's Riddle exemplified, and that great promise, Rom. 8.28, verified. Out of the eater comes forth meat, and sweetness out of the strong" (N xiv).

Rhythm of the New: "That night we had a mess of wheat for our supper" (N 22).

The trick of her text is its mix.

* * *

> At last, after many weary steps I saw *Wachuset* hills, but many miles off. Then we came to a great *Swamp*, through which we travelled up to the knees, in mud and water, which was very heavy going to one tyred before. Being almost spent, *I* thought I should have sunk down at last, and never gat out, but *I* may say as in *Psal.* 94.18, *When my foot slipped, thy mercy,* O *Lord held me up*. Going along, having indeed my life, but little spirit, *Philip*, who was in the Company, came up and took me by the hand. (N 46–47)

King Philip, Increase Mather's "perfidious and bloody Author of the War," helped Mary Rowlandson climb out of mud and water. When she was an author she remembered to write it.

Her view of King Philip's War and her picture of Metacomet himself is a contradiction of orthodox Puritan history.

One moral sense soon cancels another in a country of progress and force.

> Thereupon he [Metacomet/Philip] betook himself to flight, but as he was coming out of the Swamp, an English-man and an Indian endeavored to fire at him, the English-man missed of his aime, but the Indian shot him through the heart, so as that he fell down dead. . . . This Wo was brought upon him that spoyled when he was not spoyled. And in that very place where he first contrived and began his mischief, was he taken and destroyed, and there was he (Like as Agag was hewed in pieces before the Lord) cut into four quarters, and is now hanged up as a monument of revenging Justice, his head being cut off and carried away to Plymouth, his Hands were brought to *Boston*. . . . Thus did God break the head of that Leviathan, and gave it to be meat to the people inhabiting the wilderness, and brought it to the town of *Plimouth* the very day of their solemn Festival. (BH 139–40)

This was in 1676. Wootonokanuske, Philip's wife, had been captured earlier that year with their nine-year-old son. They were both sold into slavery and so vanish from history.

On August 6, Weetamoo, sachem of the Pocasset Wampanoags, Quannopin's wife, and Mary Rowlandson's mistress during her captivity, was betrayed by one of her subjects. This deserter led twenty English soldiers to her camp near the Taunton River. Weetamoo was drowned while trying to escape on a raft. Later her body washed up in Metapoiset. The English who found this newly dead body didn't know who it was but cut off the head anyway and stuck it on a pole in Taunton. Some Indian prisoners there "knew it presently, and made a most horrid and diabolical Lamentation, crying out it was their Queens head" (BH 138).

Quannopin was captured August 16, 1676, and taken to Newport, Rhode Island, where he was tried by court-martial August 24. The next day the chief war sachem of the Narragansetts and Mary Rowlandson's former master was executed with his brother Sunkeejunasuc.

* * *

"Oh! the wonderful power of God that mine eyes have seen, affording matter enough for my thoughts to run in, that when others are sleeping, mine eyes are weeping.

I *have seen the extrem vanity of this World*" (N 72).

* * *

She came tumbling onto the American trail with the smell of death in her nostrils and the sound of women wailing for their children.

"Go to Shiloh, and see what I did to it, for the wickedness of my People Israel. Go, and view it" (RS 143–44).

Mary Rowlandson saw what she did not see said what she did not say.

Key

AB *The Complete Works of Anne Bradstreet*: McElrath and Robb, eds.
AC *The Antinomian Controversy*: David D. Hall, ed.
AT *An American Triptych*: Wendy Martin.
BH *A Brief History*: Increase Mather.
CW *The Complete Works of Ralph Waldo Emerson.*
K *A Key into the Language of America*: Roger Williams.
LCP *Language, Counter-Memory, Practice*: Michel Foucault.
M *Magnalia Christi Americana*: Cotton Mather.
MD *Mary Dyer of Rhode Island*: Horatio Rogers.
N *The Narrative of Mary Rowlandson.*
O *Otherwise than Being or Beyond Essence*: Emmanuel Levinas.
QC *The Quakers in the American Colonies*: Rufus Jones.
R *Records of the First Church*: Richard D. Pierce, ed.
RD "John Winthrop Writes His Journal": Richard S. Dunn.
RS Rev. Joseph Rowlandson's "Sermon."

WJ *Winthrop's Journal, "History of New England, 1630–1649"*: James Kendall Hosmer, ed.
WH *The History of New England from 1630 to 1649*: John Winthrop; James Savage, ed.
WP *Winthrop Papers* Vol. 5, 1645–1649: Allyn B. Forbes, ed.
WWP *Wonder-Working Providence*: Edward Johnson.

Sources

Bradstreet, Anne. *The Complete Works of Anne Bradstreet*. Edited by Joel R. McElrath and Allan J. Robb. Boston: Twayne Publishers, 1981.

Dunn, Richard S. "John Winthrop Writes His Journal." *William and Mary Quarterly*, 41:2 (April 1984), 185–212.

Emerson, Ralph Waldo. *The Complete Works of R. W. Emerson*. Vol. 11, *Miscellanies*. Boston: Houghton-Mifflin, 1878.

Foucault, Michel. *Language, Counter-Memory, Practice: Selected Essays and Interviews*. Edited by Donald F. Bouchard. Ithaca, N.Y.: Cornell University Press, 1977.

Greene, David L. "New Light on Mary Rowlandson." *Early American Literature* 20 (1985), 24–38.

Hall, David D., ed. *The Antinomian Controversy, 1632–1638: A Documentary History*. Middletown, Conn.: Wesleyan University Press, 1968.

Johnson, Edward. *Wonder-Working Providence of Sions Savior in New-England*. 1654. Reprint. Delmar, N.Y.: Scholars Facsimile and Reprints, 1974.

Jones, Rufus M. *The Quakers in the American Colonies*. London: Macmillan, 1911.

Levinas, Emmanuel. *Otherwise than Being or Beyond Essence*. Translated by Alphonso Lingis. The Hague: Martinus Nijhoff Philosophy Texts, Vol. 3., 1981.

Martin, Wendy. *An American Triptych: Anne Bradstreet, Emily Dickinson, Adrienne Rich*. Chapel Hill: University of North Carolina Press, 1984.

Mather, Cotton. *Magnalia Christi Americana: or, The Ecclesiastical History of New-England*. 2 vols. Hartford, Conn.: Silas Andrus & Son, 1855.

Mather, Increase. *A Brief History of the Warr with the Indians in New-England . . . Together with a Serious Exhortation to the Inhabitants of That Land*. Reprinted in *So Dreadfull a Judgment: Puritan Responses to King Philip's War, 1676–1677*. Edited by Richard Slotkin and James K. Folsom. Middletown, Conn.: Wesleyan University Press, 1978.

The Records of the First Church in Boston, 1630–1868. Edited by Richard D. Pierce. *Publications of the Colonial Society of Massachusetts*. Collections, vol. 39. Boston: The Society, 1961.

Rogers, Horatio. *Mary Dyer of Rhode Island: The Quaker Martyr that was hanged on Boston Common, June 1st, 1660*. Providence, R.I.: Preston and Rounds, 1896.

Rowlandson, Mary. *The Narrative of the Captivity and Restoration of Mrs. Mary Rowlandson. First printed in 1682 at Cambridge, Massachusetts, & London, England. Now reprinted in facsimile; Whereunto are annexed a map of her removes, biographical and historical notes, and the last sermon of her husband, Rev. Joseph Rowlandson*. Edited by Henry Stedman Nourse and John Eliot Thayer. Lancaster, Mass.: 1903.

Rowlandson, Joseph. See above.

Thoreau, Henry D. *A Week on the Concord and Merrimack Rivers*. Cambridge, Mass.: Riverside Press, Houghton Mifflin, 1890.

Williams, Roger. *A Key into the Language of America*. 1643. Reprint. Providence, R.I.: Roger Williams Press, for the Rhode Island and Providence Plantations Tercentenary Committee, 1936.

Winthrop, John. *The History of New England from 1630 to 1649*. 2 vols. Edited by James Savage. Boston: Phelps and Farnham, 1825.

———. *Winthrop Papers*. Vol. 5, 1645–1649. Edited by Allyn B. Forbes. Boston: Massachusetts Historical Society, 1941.

———. *Winthrop's Journal, "History of New England," 1630–1649*. 2 vols. Edited by James Kendall Hosmer. New York: C. Scribner's Sons, 1908.

These Flames and Generosities of the Heart

Emily Dickinson and the Illogic of Sumptuary Values

Spirit cannot be moved by Flesh—It must be moved by spirit—
It is strange that the most intangible is the heaviest—but Joy and Gravitation have their own ways. My ways are not your ways—

(L pf44)

An idea of the author Emily Dickinson—her symbolic value and aesthetic function—has been shaped by *The Poems of Emily Dickinson; Including variant readings critically compared with all known manuscripts*, edited by Thomas H. Johnson and first published by the Belknap Press of Harvard University in 1951, later digested into a one-volume edition, to which I do not refer because of Johnson's further acknowledged editorial emendations. For a long time I believed that this editor had given us the poems as they looked. Nearly forty years later, *The Manuscript Books of Emily Dickinson*, edited by R. W. Franklin and again published by the Belknap Press of Harvard University, Cambridge, Massachusetts, and London, in 1981, and *The Master Letters of Emily Dickinson*, also edited by R. W. Franklin, in 1986, this time published by the Amherst College Press, show me that in a system of restricted exchange, the subject-creator and her art in its potential gesture were domesticated and occluded by an assumptive privileged Imperative.

* * *

A Concrete Community of Exchange Among Peers

1951: "1860: Alignment of words less regular, letters in a word sometimes diminishing in size toward the end, which gives an uneven effect to the page. *No important changes in form*" [my italics.] (PED liv).

1986: "Standard typesetting conventions have also been followed in regard to spacing and punctuation. No attempt has been made to indicate the amount of space between words, or between words and punctuation, or to indicate, for example, the length of a dash, its angle, spatial relation to adjoining words or distance from the line of inscription. Dashes of any length are represented by an en dash, spaced on each side. Periods, commas, question marks, ending quotation marks, and the like, have no space preceding them, however situated in the manuscripts. Stray marks have been ignored." (ML 10)

* * *

Fellows

1958: Thomas H. Johnson: Introduction to *The Letters of Emily Dickinson.*

> Since Emily Dickinson's full maturity as a dedicated artist occurred during the span of the Civil War, the most convulsive era of the nation's history, one of course turns to the letters of 1861–1865, and the years that follow, for her interpretation of events. But the fact is that she did not live in history and held no view of it past or current (L xx).

1986: Ralph W. Franklin: Introduction to *The Master Letters.*

> Dickinson did not write letters as a fictional genre, and these were surely part of a much larger correspondence yet unknown to us. In the earliest one, written when both she and the Master were ill, she is responding to his initiative after a considerable silence. The tone, a little distant but respectful and gracious, claims few prerogatives from their experience, nothing more than the license to be concerned about his health. . . . The other two letters, written a few years later, stand in impassioned contrast to this. . . . In both she defends herself, reviewing their history, asserting her fidelity. She asks what he would do if she came "in white." She pleads to see him. (ML 5)
>
> A drop of ink mars the top of the third page [first letter], but it may have come after she had written *an awkward predication* [my italics] further down the same page:
>
> Each Sabbath on the
> sea, makes me count

the Sabbaths, till we
will the
meet on shore – and
whether the hills will
look as blue as the
sailors say–

This would require obstrusive correction, and what was to have been a final draft became an intermediate one (ML 11).

1951: T. H. Johnson: Introduction to Emily Dickinson's *Collected Poems*, called "Creating the Poems: The Poet and the Muse."

It would thus appear that when Emily Dickinson was about twenty years old her latent talents were invigorated by a gentle, grave young man [Benjamin Franklin Newton] who taught her how to observe the world. . . . Perhaps during the five years after Newton's death she was trying to fashion verses in a *desultory* manner. Her muse had left the land and she must await the coming of another. That event occured in 1858 or 1859 in the person of the Reverend Charles Wadsworth. . . . A volcanic commotion is becoming apparent in the emotional life of Emily Dickinson. . . . Except to her sister Lavinia, who never saw Wadsworth, she talked to no one about him. That fact alone establishes the place he filled in the structure of her emotion. Whereas Newton as muse had awakened her to a sense of her talents, Wadsworth as muse made her a poet. The Philadelphia pastor, now forty-seven, was at the zenith of his mature influence, fifteen years married and the head of a family, an established man of God whose rectitude was unquestioned. . . . By 1870 . . . [t]he crisis in Emily Dickinson's life was over. Though nothing again would wring from her the anguish and the fulfillment of the years 1861–1865, she continued to write *verses* throughout her life. [my italics] (PED xxi–iv)

1971: *Webster's Third New International Dictionary*.

VERSE: 3 a (1): metrical language: speech or writing distinguished from ordinary language by its distinctive patterning of sounds and esp. by its more pronounced or elaborate rhythm. (2): metrical writing that is distinguished from poetry esp. by its lower level of intensity and its lack of essential conviction and commitment. ⟨many writers of ~ who have not aimed at writing poetry—T. S. Eliot⟩ (3): POETRY

2⟨~ ~ that gives immortal youth to mortal maids—W. S. Landor⟩
4 a (1): a unit of metrical writing larger than a single line: STANZA.

* * *

Circles

In 1985 I wrote a letter to Ralph Franklin, the busy director of the Beinecke Rare Book and Manuscript Library at Yale University, to suggest that *The Manuscript Books of Emily Dickinson* show that after the ninth fascicle (about 1860) she began to break her lines with a consistency that the Johnson edition seemed to have ignored. I was interested because Franklin is currently editing the new *Poems of Emily Dickinson: Including variant readings critically compared with all known manuscripts* for Harvard University Press. I received a curt letter in response. He told me the notebooks were not artistic structures and were not intended for other readers; Dickinson had a long history of sending poems to people—individual poems—that were complete, he said. My suggestion about line breaks depended on an "assumption" that one reads in lines; he asked, "what happens if the form lurking in the mind is the *stanza*?" [my italics]

* * *

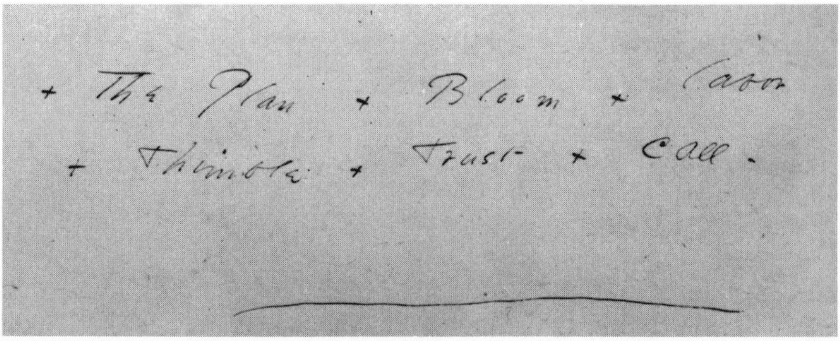

(MBED 2:1020; S3)

Thomas H. Johnson's *The Poems of Emily Dickinson* did restore the poet's idiosyncratic spelling, punctuation (the famous dashes), and word variants to her poems. At the same time he created the impression that a definitive textual edition could exist. He called his Introduction "Creating the Poems," then gave their creator a male muse-minister. He arranged her "verses" into hymnlike stanzas with little variation in form and no variation of cadence. By choosing a sovereign system for her line endings—*his* preappointed Plan—he established the constraints of a strained positivity. Copious footnotes, numbers, comparisons, and chronologies mask his authorial role.

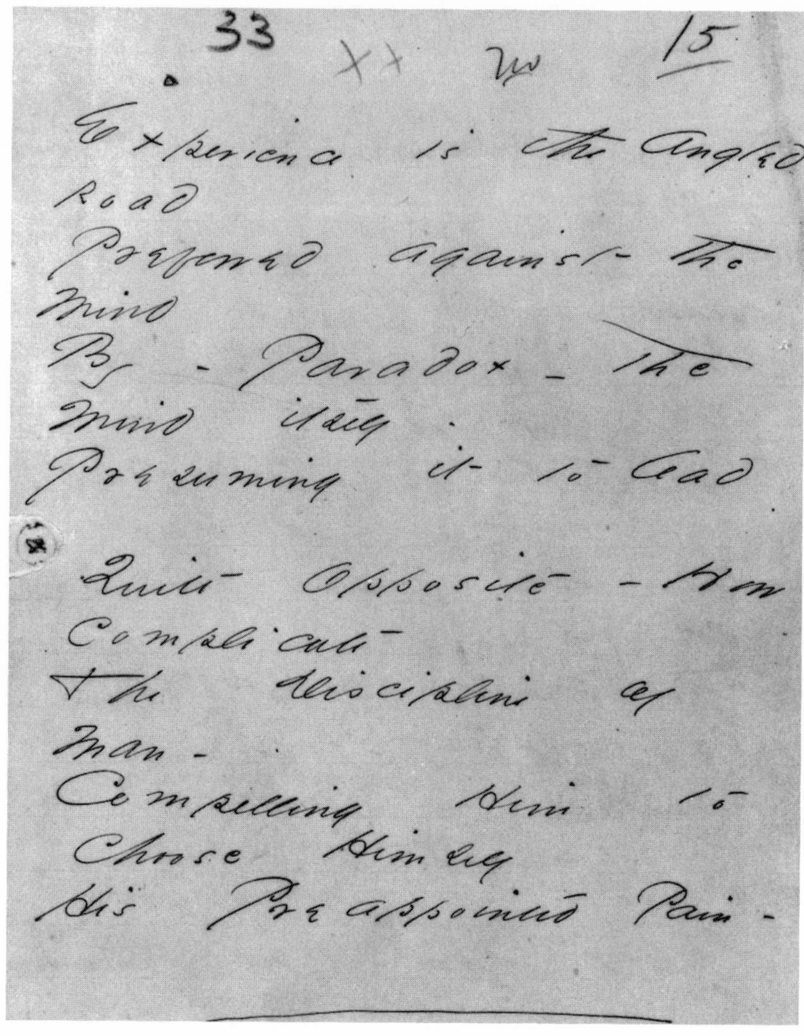

33 XX 15

Experience is the Angled
Road
Preferred against the
Mind
By - Paradox - the
Mind itself -
Presuming it to lead

Quite Opposite - How
Complicate
The Discipline of
Man -
Compelling Him to
Choose Himself
His Preappointed Pain -

(MBED 2:1033; S5)

Here is a typographical transcription of Dickinson's manuscript version:

Experience is the Angled
Road
Preferred against the
Mind
By - Paradox - The
Mind itself -
Presuming it to lead

Quite Opposite - How
Complicate
The Discipline of
Man -
Compelling Him to
Choose Himself
His Pre appointed Pain -

The Manuscript Books of Emily Dickinson complicate T. H. Johnson's criteria for poetic order.

These lines traced by pencil or in ink on paper were formed by an innovator.

This visible handwritten sequence establishes an enunciative clearing outside intention while obeying intuition's agonistic necessity.

These lines move freely through a notion of series we may happen to cross—ambiguous articulated Place.

At the end of conformity on small sheets of stationery:

When Winds hold Forests in their Paws -
+ The Firmaments - are still -
+ The Universe - is still +

(MBED 1:505; f22)

Deflagration of what was there to say. No message to decode or finally decide. The fascicles have a "halo of wilderness." By continually interweaving expectation and categories they checkmate inscription to become what a reader offers them.

Publication - is the Auction
Of the Mind of Man -
Poverty - be justifying
For so foul a thing

Possibly - but We - would
rather
From Our Garret go
White - Unto the White Creator_
Than invest - Our Snow -

Thought belong to Him who
gave it -
Then -- to Him Who bear
Its Corporeal illustration - Sell
The Royal Air -

In the Parcel - Be the Merchant
Of the Heavenly Grace -
But reduce no Human Spirit
To Disgrace of Price -

(MBED 2:915; f37)

Use value is a blasphemy. Form and content collapse the assumption of Project and Masterpiece. Free from limitations of genre Language finds true knowledge estranged in it self.

Distance - be Her only
+ Motion –
If tis Nay - or Yes -
Acquiescence - or Demurral -
Whosoever guess -

+ He - must pass the Crystal + Angle
That + obscure Her face --
He - must have achieved in
person
Equal Paradise -

+ too + Swelling + fitter for
the feet + Ever could endow –
+ claim + Signal + first + limit
+ divide -

(MBED 2:818; f34)

* * *

1991: *An editor's query.* "You need to give the reader some thoughts about making use of the words at the end of the 'poem proper' (in this case, I think, beginning with 'too swelling fitter for'). Are we to attach these words as alternatives to certain words in the 'poem'?; i.e., *where does 'too' go? What am I to do with it?*"

This is a good question: Thomas Johnson reads these words as alternatives.

1840: Noah Webster: *An American Dictionary of the English Language.**

TOO, *adv.* [Sax, *to.*]

1. Over: more than enough; noting excess; as, a thing is *too* long, *too* short, or *too* wide; *too* high; *too* many; *too* much.

His will *too* strong to bend, *too* proud to learn. *Cowley.*

2. Likewise; also; in addition.

A courtier and a patriot *too* Pope
Let those eyes that view
The daring crime, behold the vengeance *too.* Pope

3. *Too, too.* repeated, denotes excess emphatically; but this repetition is not in respectable use.

[The original application of *to*, now *too*, seems to have been to a word signifying a great quantity; as, speaking or giving *to* much; that is, *to* a great amount. *To* was thus used by old authors.] (WD 1159–60)

* * *

Rearrangement

Much critical and editorial attention has been given to Dickinson's use of capitalization and the dash in her poems and letters; while motivating factors for words and phrases she often added to a "poem proper," sometimes in the margins, sometimes between lines, but most often at the end, have aroused less interest. Since the Johnson edition was published in 1951, it has been a given of Dickinson scholarship that these words represent nothing more than suggested alternates for specific words in the text the poet had frequently marked with a cross.

Ralph Franklin says that after 1861 these possibilities for alternate readings are a part of the structure of the poems she transcribed and bound together, and his edition of *The Manuscript Books* shows this to have been the case.

*Emily Dickinson owned an 1844 reprint of Webster's 1840 edition. The family owned the 1828 two-volume first edition. Webster, a friend of the Dickinson family, was a resident of Amherst, helped to found Amherst College with Samuel Fowler Dickinson and served on the board of the Amherst Academy with Edward Dickinson.

After 1861, Dickinson's practice of variation and fragmentation also included line breaks. Unlike Franklin, I believe there is a reason for them.

This space is the poem's space. Letters are sounds we see. Sounds leap to the eye. Word lists, crosses, blanks, and ruptured stanzas are points of contact and displacement. Line breaks and visual contrapuntal stresses represent an athematic compositional intention.

This space is the poet's space. Its demand is her method.

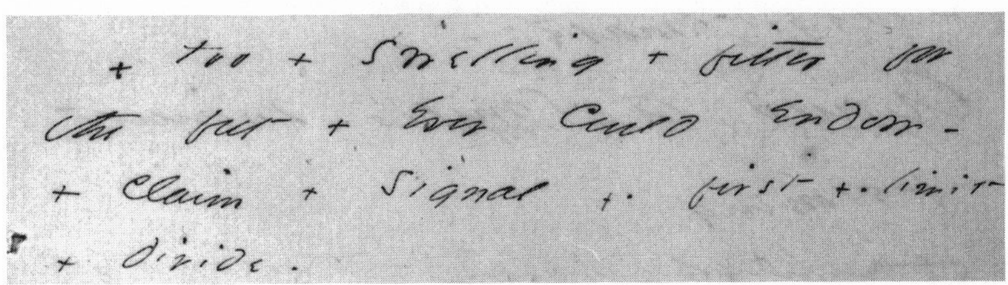

+ too + Swelling + fitter for
the feet + Ever could endow -
+ claim + Signal +. first +. limit
+ divide.

(MBED 2:818; f34)

One of Thomas Johnson's contributions to transmission of the handwritten manuscripts into print was to place these words, sometimes short phrases, at the end of a poem, as Dickinson had done. But he couldn't leave it at that. This textual scholar-editor, probably with the best intentions, matched word to counterword, numbered lines as *he* had reduplicated them, then exchanged his line numbers for her crosses.

3. True] too
6. Loaded] Swelling
13. Fitter feet – of Her] fitter for the feet
16] Ever could endow–
17. ask] claim
21. Motion] Signal
25. He] first
25. Angle] limit
26. obscure] divide –

(PED 649)

Emily Dickinson's writing is a premeditated immersion in immediacy.

Codes are confounded and converted. "Authoritative readings" confuse her nonconformity.

In 1991 these manuscripts still represent a Reformation.

* * *

Swelling

NOAH WEBSTER:

SWELL. *v.t.* To increase the size, bulk, or dimensions of; to cause to rise, dilate, or increase. Rains and dissolving snow *swell* the rivers in spring, and cause floods. Jordan is *swelled* by the snows of Mount Libanus (WD 1118).

* * *

A covenant of works

"The flood of her talent is rising" (L 332).

The production of meaning will be brought under the control of social authority.

For T. H. Johnson, R. W. Franklin, and their publishing institution, the Belknap Press of Harvard University, the conventions of print require humilities of caution.

Obedience to tradition. Dress up dissonance. Customary usage.

Provoking visual fragmentation will be banished from the body of the "poem proper."

Numbers and word matches will valorize these sensuous visual catastrophes.

Lines will be brought into line without any indication of their actual position.

An editor edits for mistakes. Subdivided in conformity with propriety.

A discreet biographical explanation: unrequited love for a popular minister will consecrate the gesture of this unconverted antinomian who refused to pass her work through proof.

Later the minister will turn into a man called "Master."

R. W. FRANKLIN: Although there is no evidence the [Master] letters were ever posted (none of the surviving documents would have been in suitable condition), they indicate a long relationship, geographically apart, in which correspondence would have been the primary means of communication (ML 5).

Poems will be called letters and letters will be called poems.

"The tone, a little distant but respectful and gracious, claims few prerogatives." (ML 5)

"*. . . the Hens*
lay finely . . ." (Epigraph to L, part 1, vol. 1)

Now she is her sex for certain for editors picking and choosing for a general reader reading.

NOMINALIST and REALIST
"Into [print] will I grind thee, my bride" (E2 241).

Franklin's facsimile edition of *The Manuscript Books of Emily Dickinson* shows some poems with so many lists of words or variants that even Johnson, who was nothing if not methodical, couldn't find numbers for such polyphonic visual complexity.

What if the author went to great care to fit these words onto pages she could have copied over? Left in place, seemingly scattered and random, these words form their own compositional relation.

R. W. EMERSON: I am very much struck in literature by the appearance that one person wrote all the books; as if the editor of a journal planted his body of reporters in different parts of the field of action, and relieved some by others from time to time; but there is such equality and identity both of judgment and point of view in the narrative that it is plainly the work of one all-seeing, all-hearing gentleman. I looked into Pope's Odyssey yesterday: it is as correct and elegant after our canon of to-day as if it were newly written (E2 232).

Antinomy. A conflict of authority. A contradiction between conclusions that seem equally logical reasonable correct sealed natural necessary

1637: Thomas Dudley at *Mrs. Ann Hutchinson's examination by the General Court at Newton*:
"What is the scripture she brings?" (AC 338)

An improper poem. Not in respectable use. Another way of reading.
Troubled subject-matter is like troubled water.

* * *

Fire may be raked up in the ashes, though not seen.

Words are only frames. No comfortable conclusion. Letters are scrawls, turnabouts, astonishments, strokes, cuts, masks.

These poems are representations. These manuscripts should be understood as visual productions.

The physical act of copying is a mysterious sensuous expression.

Wrapped in the mirror of the word.

Most often these poems were copied onto sheets of stationery previously folded by the manufacturer. The author paid attention to the smallest physical details of the page. Embossed seals in the corner of recto and verso leaves of paper are part of the fictitious real.

(MBED 1:134; f8)

(MDED 1:135; f8)

basket of flowers
C. V. Mills, capitol and, CONGRES
capitol in oval
CONGRESS above capitol
flower in oval
G & T in eight-sided device
G. & T. in oval
LEE MASS.
PARSONS PAPER CO
queen's head above L (laid)
queen's head above L (wove)
WM above double-headed eagle
(MBED 2:1411)

Spaces between letters, dashes, apostrophes, commas, crosses, form networks of signs and discontinuities.

"Train up a Heart in the way it should go and as quick as it can twill depart from it" (L pf115).

Mystery is the content. Intractable expression. Deaf to rules of composition.

What is writing but continuing.

Who knows what needs she has?

The greatest trial is trust.

Fire in the heart overcomes fire without

* * *

Franklin's notes to set 7 tell us: "On her inventory of the manuscripts obtained from her mother [Mabel Loomis Todd], MTB [Millicent Todd Bingham] recorded a small slip laid inside sheet A 86-¾ bearing only the word 'Augustly!' The paper is wove, cream, and blue-ruled." (MBED 2:1387)

* * *

Disjunct Leaves

Emily Dickinson almost never titled a poem.

She titled poems several times.

She drew an ink slash at the end of a poem.

Sometimes she didn't.

She seldom used numbers to show where a word or a poem should go.

She sometimes used numbers to show where a word or a line should go.

The poems in packets and sets can be read as linked series.

The original order of the packets was broken by her friends and first editors so that even R. W. Franklin—the one scholar, apart from the Curator of Manuscripts, allowed unlimited access to the originals at Harvard University's Houghton Library—can be absolutely sure only of a particular series order for poems on a single folded sheet of stationery.

Maybe the poems in a packet were copied down in random order, and the size of letter paper dictated a series; maybe not.

When she sent her first group of poems to T. W. Higginson, she sent them separately but together.

She chose separate poems from the packets to send to friends.

Sometimes letters are poems with a salutation and signature.

Sometimes poems are letters with a salutation and signature.

If limits disappear where will we find bearings?

What were her intentions for these crosses and word lists?

If we could perfectly restore each packet to its original order, her original impulse would be impossible to decipher. The manuscript books and sets preserve their insubordination. They can be read as events, signals in a pattern, relays, inventions or singular hymnlike stanzas.

T. W. Higginson wrote in his "Preface" to *Poems by Emily Dickinson* (1890): "The verses of Emily Dickinson belong emphatically to what Emerson long since called 'The Poetry of the Portfolio,'—something produced absolutely without the thought of publication, and solely by way of the writer's own mind. . . . They are here published as they were written, with very few and superficial changes; although it is fair to say the titles have been assigned, almost invariably, by the editors" (P iii–v).

But the poet's manuscript books and sets had already been torn open. Their contents had been sifted, translated, titled, then regrouped under categories called, by her two first editor-"friends": "Life," "Love," "Nature," "Time and Eternity."

* * *

White lines on a white stone

On September 12, 1840, Ralph Waldo Emerson wrote to Elizabeth Hoar: "My chapter on 'Circles' begins to prosper, and when it is October I shall write like a Latin Father" (E I 433*n*).

"The one thing which we seek with insatiable desire is to forget ourselves, to be surprised out of our propriety, to lose our sempiternal memory and to do something without knowing how or why; in short to draw a new circle. Nothing great was ever achieved without enthusiasm. The way of life is wonderful; it is by abandonment" (E I 321).

* * *

Overflow

1891: Twenty years after the event, T. W. Higginson, with Mabel Loomis Todd, the first editor of Emily Dickinson's poetry, recalled one of his two meetings with the poet.

> The impression undoubtedly made on me was that of an excess of tension, and of an abnormal life. Perhaps in time I could have got beyond that somewhat overstrained relation which not my will, but her needs had forced upon us. Certainly I should have been most glad to bring it down to the level of simple truth and every-day comradeship; but it was not altogether easy (L 342b*n*).

TOO. *adv.* [Sax. *to.*]
Over; more than enough; noting excess; as, a thing is *too* long, *too* short, *too* wide, *too* high, *too* many, *too* much (WD 1159).

* * *

Coming to Grips with the World

In 1986, Ralph Franklin sent me a copy of *The Master Letters of Emily Dickinson*, published by the Amherst College Press. Along with *The Manuscript Books*, this is the most important contribution to Dickinson scholarship I know of. In this edition, Franklin decided on a correct order for the letters, showed facsimiles, and had them set in type on each facing page, with the line breaks as she made them. I wrote him a letter again suggesting that if he broke the lines here according to the original text, he might consider doing the same for the poems. He thanked me for my "immodest" compliments and said he had broken the letters line-for-physical-line only to make reference to the facsimiles easier; if he were editing a book of the letters, he would use run-on treatment, as there is no expected genre form for prose. He told me there is such a form for poetry, and he intended to follow it, rather than accidents of physical line breaks on paper.

* * *

As a poet, I cannot assert that Dickinson composed in stanzas and was careless about line breaks. In the precinct of Poetry, a word, the space around a word, each letter, every mark, silence, or sound volatizes an inner law of form—moves on a rigorous line.

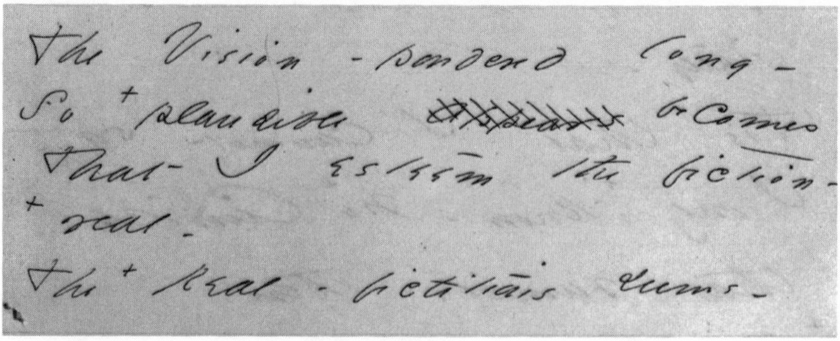
The Vision - pondered long -
So +plausible becomes
That I esteem the fiction -
+ real -
The + Real - fictitious seems -

(MBED 2:815; f34)

I wonder at Ralph Franklin's conclusion that these facsimiles are not to be considered as artistic structures.

How can this meticulous editor, whose acute attention to his subject matter has yet to be deciphered in the neutralized reading even her fervent admirers give her, now repress the physical immediacy of these spiritual improvisations he has brought to light?

A Man may +make
a Remark -
In itself - a +quiet thing
That may furnish + the
Fuse unto a Spark
In dormant nature - lain -

Let us +divide - with
skill -
Let us +discourse - with
care -
Powder exists in +Charcoal -
Before it +exists in
Fire -

\+ drop + tranquil + ignition
\+ deport + disclose
\+ Elements - sulphurets
\+ express

(MBED 2:1047; s5)

Simple reflection should cast light on the inauthentic nostalgia of *A Portrait of the Artist as a Woman*, isolated from historical consciousness, killing time for no reason but arbitrary convenience, as she composes, transcribes, and arranges into notebooks or sets over a thousand visionary works.

During her lifetime this writer refused to collaborate with the institutions of publishing. When she created herself author, editor, and publisher, she situated her production in a field of free transgressive prediscovery.

It is over a hundred years after her death; if I am writing a book and I quote from one of her letters or poems and use either the Johnson or Franklin edition of her texts, I must obtain permission from and pay a fee to

> The President and Fellows of Harvard College
> and the Trustees of Amherst College.

"is this the Hope that opens and shuts, like the eye of the Wax Doll?

Your Scholar—" (L 553)

"This is the World that opens and shuts, like the Eye of the Wax Doll—"

(L 554)

* * *

+ Drop + Tranquil + Ignition
+ Deport + Disclose
+ Elements - Sulphurets
+ Express

(MBED 2:1047; S5)

Poetry is never a personal possession. The poem was a vision and gesture before it became sign and coded exchange in a political economy of value. At the moment these manuscripts are accepted into the property of our culture their philosopher-author escapes the ritual of framing—symmetrical order and arrangement. Are all these works poems? Are they fragments, meditations, aphorisms, events, letters? After the first nine fascicles, lines break off interrupting meter. Righthand margins perish into edges sometimes tipped by crosses and calligraphic slashes.

This World is not Conclusion -
A + Species stands beyond
Invisible , as Music
But positive , as Sound -
It beckons , and it baffles -
Philosophy - dont know -
And through a Riddle, at the last
Sagacity , must go -
To +guess it , puzzles scholars -
To gain it Men have borne
Contempt of Generations
And Crucifixion , shown -
Faith slips and laughs, and rallies
Blushes, if any see
Plucks at a twig of Evidence
And asks a Vane, the way -
Much Gesture from the
Pulpit -
Strong + Hallelujahs roll -
Narcotics cannot still the
Tooth
That nibbles at the soul -

\+ A sequel - + prove it -
\+ Sure + Mouse - .

(MBED 1:396–97; f18)

Define the bounds of naked Expression. *Use.*

All scandalous breakings out are thoughts at first. Resequenced. Shifted. Excluded. Lost.

"She reverted to pinning slips to sheets to maintain the proper association" (MBED p1413).

Oneness and scattering.

Marginal notes. Irretrievable indirection—

Uncertainty extends to the heart of replication. Meaning is scattered at the limit of concentration. The other of meaning is indecipherable variation.

In his preface to *The Poems of Emily Dickinson*, called "Creating the Poems," T. H. Johnson referred to her "fear of publication," as many others have done other since. He called her poems "effusions." During the 1860s, "[h]er creative energies were at flood, and she was being overwhelmed by forces which she could not control" (PED xviii).

"Over; more than enough; noting excess; as, a thing is *too* long, *too* short, *too* high, *too* many, *too* much" (WD 1159).

So we must meet apart -
You there - I - here -
With just the Door ajar
That Oceans are - and Prayer -
And that White + Sustenance -
Despair -   + Exercise - Privilege -

(MBED 2:797; F33)

Wayward Puritan. Charged with enthusiasm. Enthusiasm is antinomian.

431

$ 4

The Sea said
"Come" to the Brook -
The Brook said
"Let me grow" -
The Sea said
"Then you will
be a Sea" -
"I want a Brook -
Come now" -
The Sea said
"Go" to the Sea.
The Sea said
"I am he
You cherished" -
"Learned Waters -
Wisdom is stale
to Me" ———

(MBED 2:1342; S11 "about 1871")

Key

AC	*The Antinomian Controversy*: David Hall, ed.
E1	*Essays by Ralph Waldo Emerson* (First Series).
E2	*Essays by Ralph Waldo Emerson* (Second Series).
L	*The Letters of Emily Dickinson*: Johnson and Ward, eds. (pf, prose fragment)
MBED	*The Manuscript Books of Emily Dickinson*: R. W. Franklin, ed. (f, fascicle; s, set)
ML	*The Master Letters of Emily Dickinson*: R. W. Franklin, ed.
P	*Poems by Emily Dickinson*: Todd and Higginson, eds.
PED	*The Poems of Emily Dickinson*: Thomas H. Johnson, ed.
WD	*An American Dictionary of the English Language*: Noah Webster.

Sources

Emily Dickinson. *The Letters of Emily Dickinson.* 3 vols. Edited by Thomas H. Johnson and Theodora Ward. Cambridge, Mass.: The Belknap Press, Harvard University Press, 1958.

———. *The Manuscript Books of Emily Dickinson.* 2 vols. Edited by R. W. Franklin. Cambridge, Mass.: The Belknap Press, Harvard University Press, 1981.

———. *The Master Letters of Emily Dickinson.* Edited by R. W. Franklin. Amherst, Mass.: Amherst College Press, 1986.

———. *Poems by Emily Dickinson.* Edited by Mabel Loomis Todd and T. W. Higginson. Boston: Roberts Brothers, 1891.

———. *The Poems of Emily Dickinson.* 3 vols. Edited by Thomas H. Johnson. Cambridge, Mass.: The Belknap Press of Harvard University Press, 1951.

Emerson, Ralph Waldo. *Essays by Ralph Waldo Emerson.* First Series. Boston and New York: Riverside Press, Houghton Mifflin, 1865.

———. *Essays by Ralph Waldo Emerson.* Second Series. Boston and New York: Riverside Press, Houghton Mifflin, 1876.

Hall, David D., ed. *The Antinomian Controversy, 1636–1638: A Documentary History*. Middletown, Conn.: Wesleyan University Press, 1968.

Webster, Noah. *An American Dictionary of the English Language.* Revised and enlarged by Chauncey A. Goodrich. Springfield, Mass.: George and Charles Merriam, 1852.

———. *Webster's Third New International Dictionary of the English Language Unabridged.* Edited by Philip Babcock Gove, Ph.D., and the Merriam Webster editorial staff. Springfield, Mass.: G. & C. Merriam Company, 1971.

Notes

My title is the seven last words of Emerson's essay called "Circles."

"'A man,' said Oliver Cromwell, 'never rises so high as when he knows not whither he is going.' Dreams and drunkenness, the use of opium and alcohol are the semblance and counterfeit of this oracular genius, and hence their dangerous attraction for men. For the like reason they ask the aid of wild passions, as in gaming and war, to ape in some manner these flames and generosities of the heart" (EI 322).

I have tried to match the poems in type, as nearly as possible, to the Franklin edition of *The Manuscript Books*. In translating Dickinson's handwriting into type I have *not* followed standard typesetting conventions. I *have* paid attention to space between handwritten words. I *have* broken the lines exactly as she broke them. I *have* tried to match the spacing between words in the lists at the end of poems. I have not been able to pay attention to spaces between letters. I think that in the later poetry such spacing is a part of the meaning. Dickinson's frequent use of the dash was noted in the Johnson edition, but he regularized these marks. I know that in some books printed during the nineteenth century, variant readings were sometimes supplied at the end of a page, and they were marked by a sort of cross. *The History of New England from 1630 to 1649*, by John Winthrop, edited by James Savage, and published in Boston in 1826, is a good example of such practice; however, if there were more than two words, a number was used for the second one, and in other books the number of crosses increased for each word. Emily Dickinson had enough humor to read these variants as found poems. She was her own publisher and could do as she liked with her texts. These were the days of Edward Lear and Lewis Carroll; liberties were taken in print.

The bottom of a page of the Savage edition of Winthrop's *History* looked like this:

> some other place, which they both consented to, but still the
> difficulty remained; for those three, who pretended themselves
> ||conferred|| ||2step|| ||3we|| ||4taking|| ||5her||
> 39 VOL. I.
>
> Reason 2. All punishments ought to be just, and, offences varying so much in their merit by occasion of circumstances, it would be unjust to inflict the same punishment upon the least as upon the greatest.
> ||theft|| ||2presumptuous||

These manuscript books and sets represent the poet's "letter to the world." The discovery of these packets and sets galvanized her sister Lavinia into action. If Dickinson sent some of the poems in letters to friends, she also left these packets in a certain order. It is doubtful, to say the least, whether her various correspondents would have bothered to collect and then publish her poem-letters.

I have followed Johnson's choices for capitals, although I feel I could argue with his choices at times. I have been allowed access only to the originals of two manuscript books, and as a result I wouldn't dare to. In a review of *The Poems of Emily Dickinson*, published in the Boston *Public Library Quarterly*, July 1956, the poet Jack Spicer suggested such marks might have been meant as signs "of stress and tempo stronger than a comma and weaker than a period." The new critical edition must reconsider such questions. In the early fascicles, Dickinson frequently uses exclamation marks. Around fascicles 6–12, as she begins to break her lines in a new way and to regularly insert variant words into the structure of her work, nervous and repetitive exclamation marks change to the more abstract and sweeping dash. Sometimes the way she crosses her *t*'s (and this no printed version could match) seems to influence the length of the direction of the dash. The crosses she added to her texts when she included variant word possibilities should also be translated into print. The most frequent argument in favor of Johnson's changing the line breaks is the assumption that Dickinson (thrifty Yankee spinster) broke her lines at the righthand margin because of the size of the paper she was using. In other words, she ran out of space and wanted to save paper. Close examination of the Franklin Manuscript Edition shows that she could have put words onto a line had she wished to; in some cases she did crowd words onto a line. As she went on working, Dickinson increased the space between words and eventually the space between letters. If you follow Johnson's edition, you get the idea that there was no change in form from the first poem in fascicle 1 to the last poems in the sets.

In the long run, the best way to read Dickinson is to read the facsimiles, because her calligraphy influences her meaning. However, Franklin's edition is far too expensive for most people, and then there is the added difficulty of reading handwriting. I think her poems need to be transcribed into type, although increasingly I wonder if this is possible. If the cost of *The Manuscript Books* is prohibitive, what would an edition of the *Collected Letters* cost? Can the later letters and poems be separated into different categories? I am a poet, not a textual scholar. In 1956, Spicer wrote: "The reason for the difficulty of drawing a line between the poetry and prose of Emily Dickinson is that she did not wish such a line to be drawn. If large portions of her correspondence are considered not as mere letters—and indeed, they seldom communicate information, or have much to do with the person to whom they were written—but as experiments in a heightened prose combined with poetry, a new approach to her letters opens up." He based his opinion on careful examination of the letters and poems owned by the Boston Public Library.

For its time the Johnson edition was a necessary contribution to any Dickinson scholarship. It radically changed the reading of her poetry. I can't imagine my life as a poet without it. But as Emerson wrote in "Circles," "The universe is fluid and volatile. Permanence is but a word of degrees. . . . Our culture is the predominance of an idea which draws after it this train of cities and institutions. Let us rise into another idea; they will disappear." A lot has changed in poetry and in academia since 1951. The crucial advance for Dickinson textual scholarship was Ralph Franklin's facsimile edition of *The Manuscript Books*. Now the essentialist practice of traditional Dickinson textual scholarship needs to acknowledge the way these texts continually open inside meaning to be rethought. In a Dickinson poem or letter there is always something other.

Cristianne Miller, in *Emily Dickinson: A Poet's Grammar* (1987, Harvard University Press), discusses Dickinson's use of Noah Webster's introductory essay to his *American Dictionary*. Paula Bennet, in *Emily Dickinson: Woman Poet* (1990, Harvester Wheatsheaf, Key Women Writer Series), has kept to Dickinson's lineation and her method of indicating the variants with a cross, as long as she has been able to work from poems in the facsimile edition. Martha Nell Smith discusses the problem of textual meddling with Dickinson's letters to Susan Gilbert Dickinson, in "To Fill a Gap" (*San Jose Studies* 13, 1987). I am looking forward to Sharon Cameron's forthcoming book, with the wonderful title *Choosing Not Choosing*, about the manuscript books. Marta Werner is currently at work on a group of late letter-poems. These scholars are showing new directions for Dickinson scholarship.

Talisman Interview, with Edward Foster

EF: I gather from what you said earlier that you are very concerned with the idea of a distinctive American voice.

SH: I don't know why I'm so concerned about it. I don't know why I have this obsession. I think it began with my close reading of Emily Dickinson's writing. It's where thinking about her poetry and her letters led me. Her writing is infinitely open. It's like Shakespeare—a miracle. To this day I can be utterly surprised by something new I find in it, or I can be comforted by familiar beauties there. The same way passages in the Bible soothe and comfort, or some music does. Her poems and her middle and later letters encompass whatever I want to bring to them. Need to bring to them. I often worry that I may be imposing my particular obsessions on her. Then Melville means nearly as much to me. Although I don't think of him as a comforter. These two writers couldn't possibly be English. Why? This is a question that I feel obliged to try to answer.

So when you say place doesn't matter, I think it does.

EF: And so, in a way, do I. What I was talking about earlier was Jack Spicer's idea that poetry in a sense preceded language and preceded voice, that it came, as he said, from East Mars and the poet was in that sense a transmitter of the poem and, of course, would have his or her unique vocabulary through which the poem would emerge. But I think that essentially he was suggesting at times that you read through the language to locate the poem. I seem to sense that what you are saying here is that the poem in some way is the voice and that it is distinctive.

Talisman magazine, no. 4 (Spring 1990). Editor: Edward Foster; Associate editors: Joseph Donahue, Zoë English, Elaine D. Foster, Theodore Kharpertian, Joel Lewis. This interview was conducted in July 1989 and edited that autumn.

SH: Well, I do believe that Spicer radio-dictation thing, as I read it in Robin Blaser's essay on Spicer—that poetry comes from East Mars. But the outside is also a space-time phenomenon. I think the outside, or East Mars, partly consists of other people's struggles and their voices. Sounds and spirits (ghosts if you like) leave traces in a geography. It's Lawrence's sense of the spirit of the place—"Never trust the artist. Trust the tale." The tale and the place are tied in a mysterious and profound way. How did English Lawrence understand America so well? He did. So did H. D., though she left in her twenties and hardly ever returned. *The Gift* is alive with the atmosphere of Bethlehem, Pennsylvania. Space and time—America and England. Even Eliot's *Four Quartets*. Stevens says somewhere that you turn with a sort of ferocity to a place you love, to which you are essentially native. The more you try to catch at the particulars in a writer, the more particulars you think you have found, the farther you get from where you thought you were supposed to be going. I am finally learning to let myself drift. But there are different rivers and currents to drift on. Rafts or writers are made from different materials. The difference between say Melville and Dickinson would be (apart from gender) that Melville is from one side of the Connecticut River, and she is from the other side. There *is* an amazing difference between the history of upper New York State and the history of Massachusetts. Trust the place to form the voice.

EF: Using Spicer as an example again, there's that first book, *After Lorca*, in which he takes a poem outside his language and recasts it in his own vocabulary, suggesting perhaps that the poem is somehow midway between two versions. The poem is neither Lorca's Spanish nor Spicer's California English.

SH: You're right. I wish I knew Spanish, but I don't. Being half Irish, I am sensitive to variations in the English language. Now, you would say that Spicer is where the Spanish voice of Lorca becomes the California voice of Jack Spicer. As well as translation or transmission, there is a mystery of change and assimilation in time. I always have to look back into the past for some reason. Where and how the English seventeenth-century voice becomes the seventeenth-century, the nineteenth-century and even the twentieth-century American voice.

EF: Isn't that what *My Emily Dickinson* is getting at?

SH: I didn't know that's what I was interested in until I began writing the book. First I was all caught up in her use of Dickens and Browning, then her use of Shakespeare. I really was concerned to show that she didn't write in a rapturous frenzy, that she read to write. So there is an irony here. Because although on one level I firmly believe that messages come from Mars—in Spicer's sense—on another level I don't believe it. Here I was thinking about Dickinson and English writers of her time, and I more or less happened on Mary Rowlandson's captivity narrative. And it was just a mind-boggling thing, I so nearly missed it. Anyway, I had to begin again. So I wrote the book in two distinct stages. Gradually, the book became a feeling toward this thing I'm talking about. Rilke writes, in one of the *Duino Elegies*, "Strange to see meanings that clung together once, floating away / in every direction—." This is always the way with Dickinson. She is always somewhere else. She is in many ways—and it has often been said—a seventeenth-century poet. And then again, she is so far ahead of us in 1989 that editing her seems to be a nearly impossible task. And maybe the poems must really be experienced as handwritten productions—the later ones as drawings. She abolishes categories. You just showed me Spicer's review of the Johnson edition, and Spicer saw quite clearly, in the late 1950s, the textual problems her letter-poems and poem-letters raise. You don't find this issue mentioned in the endless books now being churned out on Dickinson. All of them, including my own, to my shame, use the Johnson edition. It takes a poet to see how urgent this subject of line breaks is. But then how often do critics consider poetry as a physical act? Do critics look at the print on the page, at the shapes of words, at the surface—the space of the paper itself? Very rarely. In spite of Spicer's statement about East Mars, he knows that the messages must be written down. Messages must be seen to be heard to say.

EF: Your poems often involve some specific historical context. Were you ever interested just in history as such?

SH: I always have been. It was my favorite subject in school. When I was young, I devoured historical novels. My mother was of the generation that avidly read Sir Walter Scott. So I took her lead and plowed through several of those. My father read James Fenimore Cooper novels to us. And the now completely forgotten Captain Marryat. *Children of the New Forest* and *Masterman Ready* enthralled me. I am sure they are horribly colonialist, but when I was ten I wasn't in a position to know that. So my parents shared that enthusiasm for history, and I got it from them. I had my Napoleon phase and my Queen Elizabeth phase and for a time was very concerned to prove that Richard III was a good king after all. I will never forget my joy on first reading *The Count of Monte Cristo*. I was so lost in the story I never wanted to come back out. So history and fiction have always been united in my mind. It would be hard to think of poetry apart from history.

This is one reason Olson has been so important to me. *Call Me Ishmael* enthralled me when I first read it. If he had written nothing else, he would be dear to me for that. I think that's also true of Lawrence's *Studies in Classic American Literature* and, of course, Williams's *In the American Grain*. Another short work about writing and place and force is Simone Weil's essay "The Iliad, Poem of Might." Maybe it's the same thing here as what we are talking about with Spicer and *After Lorca*. It seems to me that as writers they were trying to understand the writers or people (in Williams's case writers and others), not to explain the work, not to translate it, but to meet the work with writing—you know, to meet in time, not just from place to place but from writer to writer, mind to mind, friend to friend, from words to words. That's what I wanted to do in *My Emily Dickinson*. I wanted to do that. Not just to write a tribute but to meet her in the tribute. And that's a kind of fusion. That is what is so dear to me about Olson's book. It's a book of love even if it does rightly discuss cannibalism.

EF: So these moments of fusion are historical. But does history ever exist outside some intellectual fusion or agreement?

SH: I think so. Of course, I know that history can be falsified, has been falsified. Still, there are archives and new ways of interpreting their uncompromising details. I am naive enough to hope the truth will out. History may be a record written by winners, but don't forget Nixon taped himself for posterity. If you are a woman, archives hold perpetual ironies. Because the gaps and silences are where you find yourself.

EF: Then you do feel history is an actuality?

SH: Yes.

EF: Against which the writer is working?

SH: In and against.

EF: Do you have any background in Marxist theory?

SH: No.

EF: Your sister described the Cambridge world in which you and she grew up as leftist [Fanny Howe, "Artobiography," in *Writing/Talks*, edited by Bob Perelman], and I was wondering if that . . .

SH: Well, I guess I wouldn't describe it quite that way. Yes, it was leftist in the sense that Democrats were considered to be leftists during the fifties. The shadow of the McCarthy hysteria was heavy over Cambridge then. And my father, unlike some others, was outspoken and very courageous. But he was a solid Truman Democrat. He worshipped the American Constitution. It really was his faith. Constitutional law and legal history were the subjects he taught. He was far from being a Marxist. My mother is more theatrical, but they basically agreed politically with each other, and their friends were probably about the same: saddened by what was happening but really pretty safe at the same time, simply because they were at a place like Harvard. Harvard, and I suppose most Ivy League universities, were more sheltered. Why this was so would be an interesting line to pursue.

Harvard was very privileged during the forties and fifties, so male. The Matthiessen book [F. O. Matthiessen, *American Renaissance: Art and Expression in the Age of Emerson and Whitman*]: an intellectual and poetic Renaissance minus Emily Dickinson. Minus Harriet Beecher Stowe. Minus Margaret Fuller. Of course, minus Frederick Douglass as well. Women weren't the only ones subtracted. It's these kinds of contradictions that get me. I know Marxist-influenced scholarship, really exciting work now being done in American Studies, has made me more conscious of such contradictions. I mean it's important to try to get under the official history of Harvard. What does *that* place represent? I can't quite so simply say I grew up in a false community—a community that fancied itself as liberal. I don't want to be so hard on it because these were honorable scholars, careful researchers, and this was their profession, and they felt it was a calling. But you see, it *was* false if you were a girl or a woman who was not content to be considered second-rate.

EF: Did you know Matthiessen and Perry Miller?

SH: My parents knew them well, although I can't remember what Matthiessen looked like—I think I was about twelve when he killed himself. My mother says he got her the job directing plays at Radcliffe and Harvard. He called her the day before he died, and they talked about the theater. Then I think a note was delivered to Kenneth Murdock, and he tried to stop him, but it was too late. We were at breakfast, and the paper was flung down on the doorstep with the headlines—and their horror. They loved him. But I didn't know why. I never knew why he had killed himself. No one ever said. That was hidden. It was swept under the rug. My mother says he had had a breakdown earlier. I think there is now a biography, but I haven't read it. I am told it's a revisionist view. We never passed that dingy hotel in Boston, where he jumped out the window, without it being pointed out. It was near the Cape Cod Expressway. I suppose it's been pulled down now. I thought of his suicide as an irrational act from out of nowhere for no reason—it was doubly frightening that way. Recently I was looking over his book on T. S. Eliot, and it is so ordered, so gentlemanly, so polite and well-meant. At the same time it misses the passion in Eliot, and the doubt. What a sad thing. I think American Studies was a relatively new academic subject then, and he contributed so much to it, even if his contribution now seems dated. The doubt he left out of his studies could not so easily be repressed. Perhaps a great sadness engulfed him.

As to Perry Miller, he was one of my parents' best friends and was always around. But how did I know him? Only as a lecherous character who drank too much. He is supposed to have been an inspiring teacher. To us daughters of professors, he was the object of great scorn because we knew that if he was at one of our houses, he would quickly get red-faced and then his hands would start wandering. His wife, Betty, who I believe did half of his research for him, was silent and shadowy. What she must have endured. But she was devoted to him. They had no children. Another thing about Perry Miller—he always wore white socks and black shoes. And the skin on his ankles, always visible above the socks, was like polished porcelain. We were all struck by it. Even my parents.

EF: Good heavens! My idol!

SH: He should be your idol. So idols have feet of clay—in this case porcelain. I can't tell you how surprised I was to find, when I was working on

Dickinson, that this man, who in real life had seemed harsh and coarse, was completely different in his written work. He was and is indispensable for any real understanding of the early history of New England, of the intellectual and religious history of America. With one major exception. While Matthiessen leaves out women, Miller leaves out Native Americans. How could he have written so many books and essays, one of them called *Errand into the Wilderness* and have left out the inhabitants? Yet after faulting him for that I come back and back to his work. I am trying to indicate how conflicted the whole thing is in my mind. These democratic ("leftist" if you like) professors of English, law, and history were politically idealistic at the same time they were elitist and sexist. One of my vivid memories of that time is when Harvard hired their first woman professor of history, and she was only hired from Oxford or Cambridge on a temporary basis, the big joke among this group of friends was how they would keep toasting her at a ceremonial dinner so she would get drunker and drunker. I don't know if they ever did or only imagined they would or what. But what I do remember is that she was presented not as a fellow scholar but as a plain prim old maid who might be made a fool of. That was it. So I mean the hypocrisy here. . . . And then even so, I have come back, and these memories almost fall away but not quite. Not quite.

My father also was fascinated by the Puritans. He wrote a book about American law called *The Garden and the Wilderness*. Now, most books about the period and place must hesitate over the word *wilderness*. Because it wasn't a wilderness to Native Americans. Still it's a resonant typological word. A necessary emblem. I remember him in his study late in the evening with his light-shade on because his eyes must have been tired from so much reading for the Holmes book and students' papers, etc., but he would be bent over some old Mather or Sewell diary for relaxation! [Mark DeWolfe Howe, *Oliver Wendell Holmes*.] They said of Increase Mather that he loved his study to a kind of excess. In the 1950s, there was my father, who felt the same way, and all I could think of was acting and boys and whatever else I thought of then. And now I have taken this long journey back through Puritan history, although I entered another way. I find myself reading about the Mathers for relaxation, and I love my study to a kind of excess. I would dearly love to sit down and show my father what I know now. We would talk about the garden and the wilderness together, and all would be well. All manner of things would be well. Yet this place I want to come home to was false to women in an intellectual sense. It was false.

EF: I had sensed that Matthiessen and Miller would be somehow there, given the nature of your work, but I hadn't realized that it was that close a professional connection—as close as that with your parents. In any case, all that immediately leads me back to Olson and *Call Me Ishmael*, which seems quite explicitly to reject Miller's kind of thought, his version of literature.

SH: *Call Me Ishmael* was written back in 1947. I would have been ten; Fanny, seven. The times I am speaking of and I think she was referring to were in the early fifties. But I think it would have been impossible to write that book had he remained in academia or more specifically in Cambridge. Olson was close to some of the people there and admired them, but to do what he did, he would have had to get away. George Butterick told me he remained close to Ellery Sedgwick, who was the very image of Boston civility.

EF: Do you have any feelings about Sedgwick's book on Melville [William Ellery Sedgwick, *Herman Melville: The Tragedy of Mind*]?

SH: I don't think it's very thrilling.

EF: I don't either.

SH: Henry Murray was an interesting Cambridge character. Olson seems to have been fond of him. In his blistering "Letter for Melville 1951," Harry Murray and Jay Leyda are mentioned favorably. I only recently ran down Murray's long essay on *Pierre*. I think he edited the Grove Press edition. He was a psychoanalyst with very odd theories. Anyway, the essay on *Pierre* has a lot of valuable information; at the same time it seems a little stale. I think the most exciting book on Melville recently is *Subversive Genealogies* [by Michael Paul Rogin]. Rogin's cross-disciplinary approach to the writing and the life cuts through that blank wall scholarship so often puts up. Families have their false fronts as universities and governments do. The Melville and Gansevoort families had theirs. Melville, like Hamlet, saw the ghost under the helmet. How do you act when you know what you know? As Olson puts it in the "Letter," "this beast hauled up out of great water was society" ["Letter for Melville 1951"]. The Leviathan. Moby. Rogin beautifully shows how Melville works in and around, for and against what he sees and says. *Subversive Genealogies: The Politics and Art of Herman*

Melville is the complete title of Rogin's book. Home, politics, and art are together here as they should be. You cannot separate an author from family, history, and ideology.

EF: I suppose a question some people might ask, then, is how you deal with a world before history, before Herodotus? With the Hittites, say? People who had a sense of chronology but for whom history as we understand it did not exist.

SH: Well, they are here too. I mean the mystery is time. The undying Hittites and Babylonians may be waiting in another chronology completely. Who knows? This summer I saw a television documentary about the astronauts who went to the moon and what they are doing now, etc. Most are high-powered salesmen. What twentieth-century America does to explorers! Only one has been freakish in the best sense, and he has been searching for Noah's ark on the top of some mountain in Tibet. But all of them in their reminiscences about their trips to the moon, twenty years ago now, all of them seem to have had an overwhelming impression of the beauty of our planet. They all said that as you got out of earth's atmosphere it was just vast darkness everywhere, vast space, pitch dark, no sound; and then far back you could see this thin clear blue, azure blue, that is the atmosphere, and then you saw our tiny little world under that thin blue veil and that is it. That's all.

EF: So the things we know aren't simply things we made up.

SH: Well, whatever they are, they're a kind of order. They're a kind of beauty, they're blue, they're light. Words are candles lighting the dark. "In the beginning was the Word, and the Word was God." I think that there has to be *some* order if only order in disorder. And words and sounds are . . . they reach up out there. A little flicker in silence . . . a signal. So that would be what for Spicer . . . but what do I know? What do any of us know?

EF: I suppose at times it seems as if history is little more than a series of justifications. And no, of course, that's not it, obviously. But if you aren't content with the surface of time, poetry is the more reliable.

SH: Poets aren't reliable. But poetry may be. I don't think you can divorce poetry from history and culture. The photographs of children during the war in Europe, when I was a small child and the Holocaust was in progress—not only the Holocaust but the deaths of millions of people in Europe and Asia—prevented me from ever being able to believe history is only a series of justifications or that tragedy and savagery can be theorized away. I've recently been editing the question-from-the-audience section of a book [*The Politics of Poetic Form: Poetry and Public Form*] that consists of lectures some of us gave for a course Charles Bernstein gave at the New School last year. Someone in the audience said, "Is anything real? I personally don't know if anything is real." In the text, in a printed bracket, there is the word *laughter*. During the real event, the audience must have laughed, and I was too preoccupied at the time to notice. When I saw *laughter* in brackets, it made me angry. There is real suffering on this little planet. I mean we can discuss whether the Hittites believed in chronology and history before Herodotus, and in Bensonhurst, Brooklyn, this month, a young African-American man was murdered by a gang of Italian-American teenagers. Where did the poison of racial hatred in America begin? Will it ever end? Why are we such a violent nation? Why do we have such contempt for powerlessness? I feel compelled in my work to go back, not to the Hittites but to the invasion or settling, or whatever current practice calls it, of *this* place. I am trying to understand what went wrong when the first Europeans stepped on shore here. They came here for some reason, something pushed them. What pushed them? Isn't it bitterly ironic that many of them were fleeing the devastation caused by enclosure laws in Britain, and the first thing they did here was to put up fences? Racism is by no means unique to America. There are things that must never be forgotten. It's not a laughing matter.

EF: Well, how then are poems related to history?

SH: I think the poet opens herself as Spicer says. You open yourself and let language enter, let it lead you somewhere. I never start with an intention for the subject of a poem. I sit quietly at my desk and let various things—memories, fragments, bits, pieces, scraps, sounds—let them all work into something. This has to do with changing order and abolishing categories. It has to do with sounds in silence. It has to do with peace.

EF: And the new order that results, it's historical?

SH: I don't understand you.

EF: Is it different from historical order or is . . .

SH: You mean is poetry an order that is distinct from historical order?

EF: Is it a different way of knowing things?

SH: Yes. It depends on chance, on randomness. So there is a difference. But history and even order is still there. I think it's the valid way, but again I could be wrong. I only really know poetry, but here I am.

EF: Some of your books begin with a prose statement, and the poems follow, and it seems that you move from the prose to fragments and bits and pieces of a text, another text.

SH: Actually, I don't. I begin with fragments and bits and pieces, and they take me to what I find, and then I write an introduction to anchor the poem. The beginning is usually the end.

EF: But in the book it occurs first.

SH: Only *The Liberties* and just recently *Eikon* have introductions that are part of the poem. I wrote introductions for *Articulation* and *Thorow*, but the poems are separate from them. It's an interesting problem though and not unlike writing an essay about a poem or an author: how to make the introduction answer the poem and not merely explain it as a footnote would do. Are they introductions or are they not?

You haven't seen *Eikon* yet [*The Bibliography of the King's Book; or, Eikon Basilike*]. There is a section in *Temblor* and *The Difficulties*, but in this poem you need to see the whole thing to get the effect. I felt when I finished the poem that it was so unclear, so random, that I was crossing into visual art in some sections and that I had unleashed a picture of violence I needed to explain to myself. The end breaks out of all form completely. You could read the last page several ways.

The Liberties is another thing. I never started by thinking I was going back to write about Stella and Swift. I was in Dublin, and my mother was very sick in the Protestant hospital in the old section of the city. There are still separate hospitals there. After I would visit her, I used to walk around the streets, and St. Patrick's Cathedral was just near. That part of the city is called The Liberties. It also is built on top of Viking ruins, and at the time there was a good deal in the press about how to save the ruins from being built over by developers. So you had the sense of life being covered up. And in the cathedral, Stella is buried under the floor near the entrance, or that's where her grave marker is. You walk over it as if there were a dog buried there. Swift's pet dog. At the same time, considering that Swift was the dean of the cathedral, it seems a flagrant gesture. A swipe at respectability. The "imitate me if you dare" aspect to Swift's character Yeats wrote that epitaph for. The subject of Swift, Stella, and Vanessa was mythic for my mother and many other Irish writers. I grew up on it. It was another Grimm's fairy tale. But real. So when I began writing this time, I was really trying to paint that part of the landscape of Dublin in words. I was trying to get the place, a foreign place that was home to my mother, on paper. I thought I could understand my mother that way—I might go back to my grandmother, who I am named after and who I loved though I never saw her that often, separated as we were by first war and always the ocean. It was interesting to find that Swift was constantly wrenched between England and Ireland when he was a small child. It helps to explain the fracturing of language in his writing. And many other things. It makes him more likable.

So I start in a place with fragments, lines and marks, stops and gaps, and then I have more ordered sections, and then things break up again. That's how I begin most of my books. I think it's what we were talking about in history as well, that the outsidedness—these sounds, these pieces of words—comes into the chaos of life, and then you try to order them and to explain something, and the explanation breaks free of itself. I think a lot of my work is about breaking free: starting free and being captured and breaking free again and being captured again.

EF: The texts that you use seem . . .

SH: It just seems that I end up with this place that I wish I could belong to and wish I could describe. But I am outside looking in.

EF: So it begins in fragments and ends in prose, and prose is a kind of convention with an expected syntax and order and shape.

SH: I hope that my prose hasn't got an expected syntax. You are making it sound more planned than it is. The content is the process, and so it changes.

EF: Did you start by reading about Hope Atherton with the intention of writing the poems in *Articulation of Sound Forms in Time*?

SH: I had already written some of the poems. It was during the time I was finishing the Dickinson book and I was so interested in captivity narratives. I wrote an essay on Mary Rowlandson, and, as I said, I found her through Dickinson. I think Rowlandson is the mother of us all. American writers, I mean. Already in 1681, the first narrative written by a white Anglo-American woman is alive with rage and contradiction. She is a prophet. She speaks for us now, in the same way that slave narratives do. She says our sin. I think she has been an unacknowledged undervoice in Thoreau, Melville, Dickinson, Hawthorne, though I can't prove it. I became totally obsessed with her, and that piece I wrote was so urgent; it is hard to explain the urgency I felt ["The Captivity and Restoration of Mrs. Mary Rowlandson," *Temblor* 2]. I was worried that I hadn't been writing poetry, and I was up in the stacks at Sterling Library searching for information on various Native American raids near Deerfield and Hadley during the French and Indian Wars. Sterling houses books that aren't used often, so it has an aura of death. These books have lost their interest. Only a few professors or library workers or the odd student on the track of something eccentric come up to the sixth floor, where American history books are. It's usually very, very quiet up there. The lights are off. In silence and semidarkness, it's mysterious. I was turning the pages of a history of Hadley, and Hope's name just caught me. It was the emblematical name. Here was this person. A man with a woman's name. He had this borderline, half-wilderness, half-Indian, insanity-sanity experience. He was a minister accompanying an army. The enemy thought he might have been God. Was he telling the truth? Had he been hiding or marching? I went home and quickly wrote the abstract pieces at the beginning. Usually I work very, very slowly, but this time the sections came fast. So then there was that section and Hope's name, and the whole thing took on a different form.

EF: Do you know Richard Slotkin's *Regeneration through Violence*?

SH: Oh yes. It's a crucial book for anyone interested in American literature. He's very good on Mary Rowlandson and wonderful on other early American frontier literature. Slotkin may have brought Native Americans and popular narratives into academic historical consciousness, as Perry

Miller did not, but basically (as with Miller) historical consciousness is still male. Anne Kibbey, Ann Douglas, Patricia Caldwell, Annette Kolodny, Amy Shrager Lang, Janice Knight, and other scholars are changing things, I hope. But I see this problem in American poetry, too, and I am beginning to realize that during my lifetime there will be no profound reordering of the situation.

When I read books about American poetry and even current discussions among poets, or at least among the poets whose work interests me, I generally read about men. Yes, Dickinson is in the canon. But she is treated as an isolated case, not as part of an ongoing influence. In poetry the line usually goes from Whitman through Stevens and Pound, on through Olson to Duncan to Creeley. Then there is the New York School—O'Hara and Ashbery, etc.,—then the Beats, Ginsberg, etc. The Objectivists narrowed down to Oppen, Reznikoff, Zukofsky. Niedecker is added to the Objectivists but always with the sense that without Zukofsky her writing would be inconceivable. Stein is brought into discussions on poetics but again as an isolated case, with influence, but somehow a break in the line. Marianne Moore, the same, an isolated phenomenon in her cocked hat at baseball stadiums. Oh, and of course, H.D. But with H.D. we must always hear of her romantic connection to Pound, Lawrence; even her friendship with W. C. Williams is presented not in terms of a shared poetics but in terms of a possible romance or rejection. And it's usually their influence on her, not her influence on them. So here, while I am trying to believe and think I do believe that genius transcends gender, sometimes I honestly wonder.

EF: There is Duncan with H.D., Ashbery with Stein.

SH: There are always exceptions. And H.D. scholarship has changed for the better due to women who are scholars and to some men as well. Robert Duncan certainly looks to H.D. as a master. But I haven't heard that much about Ashbery and Stein. I hear about Ashbery and Stevens, Ashbery and Emerson, Ashbery and O'Hara, seldom Ashbery and Stein. This is not Ashbery's fault. In fact, he is going to talk about Laura Riding in his lectures at Harvard this year. It's what critics do with him. What canonization does to everyone. Another exception is Charles Bernstein. He has always made it clear how important Stein is to his work and to his writing about writing. He is careful never to discuss what he might consider to be his history of American poetry without including Riding, Niedecker, Stein, Hejinian, Darragh, Ward, Drucker and others. But when articles are written about

Language Poetry or when fights between the various covens occur, it's usually men who do the writing and fighting.

EF: Why is that?

SH: We have been told all the reasons repeatedly now. Women have been taught for so long to be seen and not heard that you can't undo generations of conditioning in a matter of twenty years or so, etc. I wish I really knew. And the endless name dropping, the repetition of the same names over and over, is at some level anathema to what poetry taps or interprets anyway. Maybe there is in silence a far greater mystery. Maybe anger is a waste. First I wanted to fight, but now I think it's more important to just keep writing poems.

EF: There have been male poets who were obsessed with women poets. Poe, for example.

SH: What do you mean he was obsessed by women poets?

EF: When a contemporary woman poet interested him, which was often, he would do something, an official notice, a review. He would say something.

SH: And Poe is in the anthologies now, not these women. But of course, during the Victorian nineteenth century, a great deal of absolutely appalling poetry was written by women and was very popular. Douglas's *The Feminization of American Culture* has a lot about this problem. There is another seminal book in American Studies. I think Emily Dickinson's inability to get her work published during her lifetime had almost nothing to do with the fact that she was a woman and everything to do with her originality. And Whitman is simply in another league from Lydia Sigourney, Helen Hunt Jackson, or T. W. Higginson for that matter. It's no good for Women's Studies departments to pretend this isn't so. What will that solve?

EF: What are your feelings generally on feminist criticism?

SH: I am very conflicted. I am wary of separation. Women's Studies, African-American Studies, etc. It seems to me only a further way to isolate texts that should be known by everyone. But then it may be a temporary necessity. I am troubled by some feminist criticism because in its stridency it is only another bias. And in a strange sense it's still a male bias. Instead of questioning the idea of power itself, many women want to assume power. "Power corrupts. Absolute power corrupts absolutely." History certainly has shown us that. Luce Irigaray, in *This Sex Which Is Not One*, questions such issues in a truly revolutionary way. Then I think Alice Jardine's *Gynesis* should be read by every person who is interested in critical theory. And there are so many young women coming along now who take this kind of thinking as their ground, while for women of my generation there was no ground.

I think it's a pity that when it comes to work on Dickinson, almost no one is questioning the very basic problem of transcription. Editing of her poems and letters has been controlled by gentlemen of the old school and by Harvard University Press since the 1950s. Franklin's edition of *The Manuscript Books* and now *The Master Letters* should have radically changed all readings of her work [R. W. Franklin, ed. *The Manuscript Books of Emily Dickinson* and *The Master Letters*]. But they haven't. This is a feminist issue. It takes a woman to see clearly the condescending tone of these male editors when they talk about their work on the texts. But on this subject there is silence so far. And this is a revolutionary way for women to go in Dickinson criticism. Well, one of Dickinson's abilities is to escape everything. If you think you can explain a poem, she quickly shows you there is a way out of that interpretation. I think I have the best intentions when it comes to reading *The Manuscript Books*, but I often wake up in the night and think, No, I am wrong. She would not agree. She would be angry with me. It's something to do with her way of not publishing, of copying her work into packets she sewed together herself, with what she left out (numbers, titles), with what she left in (variant word listings, various marks). I think she may have chosen to enter the space of silence, a space where power is no longer an issue, gender is no longer an issue, voice is no longer an issue, where the idea of a printed book appears as a trap.

EF: Are there women whose work you feel should particularly be added to the canon?

SH: I am suspicious of the idea of a canon in the first place because to enter this canon a violation has usually been done to your work, no matter what your gender may be. And besides, the more you go into something, the more you see that the canon is only the surface, only the ghost's helmet. Not the face underneath the helmet. So why have I been complaining? What is the answer? I wish I knew.

EF: Have you seen the recent American literature anthologies that try to reform the canon?

SH: Which ones?

EF: The conventional ones for college survey courses. There are many new women . . .

SH: What depresses and alarms me about the ones I've seen is that they eliminate the work of women who have used or are using language in an experimental way. This anthology business is not just a woman's problem. Not at all. There are plenty of men who are left out of the name-dropping network. It's a brutal thing. Erasure. It's a political issue that covers a wider range than gender. Nevertheless . . .

EF: Will poems ever be read as if they were not specifically written by women or specifically written by men?

SH: I don't know.

EF: It's possible?

SH: Anything is possible. I think the lyric poem is a most compressed and lovely thing. I guess it's the highest form. And in this form I hope that sexual differences are translated, transformed, and vanish.

EF: You say that in *My Emily Dickinson*, but I think a lot of people would argue the point.

SH: Oh yes, I know. They could be right.

EF: Some people seem to feel the lyric is always about gender.

SH: In what way? What do you mean?

EF: That a poem is always in some way a statement about the way it is to be a woman in the world or a man in the world. I have a feeling that a good many feminist critics . . .

SH: Well, I am not a critic. And that's where I disagree with a good many feminist critics. I think that when you write a poem you use sounds and words outside time. You use timeless articulations. I mean the ineluctable mystery of language is something . . . it's just . . . it's like earth from the astronauts' view—that little blue film, a line floating around space sheltering all of us. And in those terms, it really doesn't matter if you are a man or a woman. We are all both genders. There is nothing more boring than stridently male poetry and stridently female poetry.

EF: In the title of your Hope Atherton book you say, "sound forms in time." Can "sound forms" be otherwise? Can they be outside time?

SH: It's a mystery to me. The astronauts say in outer space it's perfectly quiet.

EF: Where does the title come from?

SH: I think it's a definition Schoenberg gives to music. I love his writing about music and Adorno's writing about him. But then I ran across the idea in a couple of other places. I can't remember where. I think there is a definition of language in the wonderful 1828 Webster's that is almost that. But I only found that last year. Poetry is a sort of music. And then I think that the first experience we probably have of the world, just as we enter, is sound. We are slapped and we cry. Before we know what meaning is. So to be born would be to hear sound you couldn't understand. And to die is to hear sound, then silence. So it's the articulation that represents life. And Hope has that sort of experience. And Hope is in me. In all of us. Once I was driving to Buffalo alone, moving up there for the winter to teach. It was me and my car and the mountains. I had a tape of *Articulation* from a reading I had done, and I thought I would turn it on as I was passing the place near where Hope had been wandering after the raid—and it was a wonderful feeling because the sounds seemed to be pieces still in the air there. I felt I was returning them home as I drove away from home. They don't belong to me. I didn't originate them. They go back.

EF: Is time just chronology?

SH: No, I wouldn't say so. I would say space-time. It's the thing that isn't chaos. Again, I've been trying to understand some of René Thom's writing [*Mathematical Models of Morphogenesis, Structural Stability and Morphogenesis*]. This isn't easy if you never were able to pass algebra! But he writes beautifully, and his diagrams are like poems. Algebraic formulas are also articulations of sound forms in time. Thom says mathematics is a universal language; numbers have sounds. So there are these forms in space and time and in apparent chaos—formulas, patterns—but at the end of *Mathematical Models*, he seems to be saying maybe it's all a game. All you can do is move the chips around pretending that there is some kind of order.

It was because of Thom that I named my Wesleyan book *Singularities*. I was having a terrible time trying to come up with a title for that group of works together (*Articulation*, *Thorow*, and *Scattering as Behavior Toward Risk*), and Thom came to Buffalo and gave a lecture called "Singularities." In algebra a singularity is the point where plus becomes minus. On a line, if you start at x point, there is $+1$, $+2$, etc. But at the other side of the point is -1, -2, etc. The singularity (I think Thom is saying) is the point where there is a sudden change to something completely else. It's a chaotic point. It's the point chaos enters cosmos, the instant articulation. Then there is a leap into something else. *Predation* and *capture* are terms he uses constantly. I thought this was both a metaphor for Europeans arriving on this continent, where a catastrophic change then had to happen—a new sense of things on the part of the original inhabitants and the emigrants, and to the land as well. And it seemed to be a way of describing these poems of mine. They are singular works on pages, and grouped together, they fracture language; they are charged. "Singularity" was a word dear to the Puritans for other reasons.

EF: Doesn't Gödel say that mathematics involves propositions that mathematical systems themselves can't prove?

SH: It's a dizzying thought. Catastrophe theory says that there is order in catastrophe. Here is a bit from *Mathematical Models*. All printed in italics!

> *In this chapter we shall consider a field of local dynamics defined as the gradient of a potential. The term elementary catastrophe is used to designate every*

conflict situation between local regimes, minima of the potential which can occur in a stable manner in 4-dimensional space-time.

By an abuse of language, we shall sometimes use the name catastrophe for the morphology that makes it appear.

We distinguish two types of catastrophe: catastrophes of conflict and catastrophes of bifurcation.

Science! It's just the introduction to a chapter. Isn't that terrific? Emily Dickinson would have been enthralled.

EF: Your new book, or at least the parts I saw in *Temblor*, seems to be asking what an icon is [*The Bibliography of the King's Book; or, Eikon Basilike*].

SH: That poem for me is . . . When you see it together in a book, you'll see that it's a catastrophe of bifurcation. That's the perfect description. I had taught these captivity narratives at Buffalo. I thought I was going to write a book of essays in the manner of *In the American Grain*. This problem of an American voice was something I wanted to write about. I found myself with the Mathers, not the narratives. I worked on an essay called "Loss of First Love" about them. I was all caught up in it and thought it was wonderful. But it was weak. Weak because the ghosts of my father and Perry Miller just prevented me from having any confidence. To say nothing of the ghost of Increase Mather. George Butterick, who I was very close to, was very ill and in great pain with cancer. He had worked with such brilliance and devotion editing Olson's writing. His illness was very much on my mind. I really was shaken because he was so young. I came home with only the botch on the Mathers and a few other beginnings, and quite by chance, Mark gave me this book called *A Bibliography of the King's Book or, Eikon Basilike*. I was struck by the ironies implicit in the very idea of a bibliography, which is a search for origins on paper. Both George Butterick and my father worked themselves to the bone in the service of commanding and prolific figures. It was bibliographic scholarship. You must erase yourself to do such work. George's editing of Olson has to be one of the most generous gifts to poetry in my time. Priceless. I have learned, because my own writing is so concerned with gaps and spaces, words that run together, etc., that typesetters who pay any attention to such deviations from the norm are few and far between. This was the great thing about Lee Hickman's work on *Temblor*. Eric Gill said, "The mind is the arbiter of letter forms, not the tool or the material." It's easiest for publishers and editors to let the machine rule the text. Even a poet like Stevens, who seems to use such regular form, has been normalized if you look at first editions of his poems. The first editor and typographers left in spaces that resonate with the letters, and by the time of the *Collected*, those spaces had been removed. The care and sensitivity George gave to editing Olson's *writing* was heroic—in the fine sense of heroic: unselfish and daring, uncompromising. Well, I won't forget it.

So I wanted to write something filled with gaps and words tossed, and words touching, words crowding each other, letters mixing and falling away from each other, commands and dreams, verticals and circles. If it was impossible to print, that didn't matter. Because it's about impossibility anyway. About the impossibility of putting in print what the mind really sees and the impossibility of finding the original in a bibliography. The coincidence of the name Charles (then I pulled Charles Dickens into it—) was one of those accidentals that make you feel the thing was planned in advance. But the Mather essay I couldn't write is there, too. I think that the execution of Charles was a primal sin in the eyes of the Puritans who killed him. They tried to bury their guilt. As in the wonderful Hawthorne story "Roger Malvin's Burial," the body would not stay buried. Regicide. I love that word. It's of the devil's party. Kings and crosses, blasphemy, and homicide are all packed into it. This was the killing of the king, and the king was holy. The Mathers were over here, so they didn't actually do the killing, but they were of the killing party. In Guilford there is a cellar where two of the regicides were hidden. Whalley Avenue in New Haven is named for a regicide. In America the regicides were heroes—in England, villains. In this English *Bibliography of the Eikon Basilike*, you have the printing record of a book that became a relic. It has such a mysterious name. And it's supposed to be by a king. It was used as propaganda for the royalist cause, yet the *Eikon* was read and cherished as a sort of sacred relic by the common people. And Milton, who is supposed to be part of the rising of the people, wrote *Eikonoklastes* in an attempt to destroy its credibility. Somehow, all my thinking about the misediting of Dickinson's texts, George's careful editing of Charles Olson's poems, all the forgotten little captivity narratives, the now-forgotten *Eikon*, the words *Eikon*, *Eikonoklastes*, and *regicide*—all sharp vertical sounds, all came together and then split open.

EF: The words split open. But then what does the word *icon* mean?

SH: That's the thing. It's not quite *icon* because it's *Eikon*. With *Basilika* added. So it's from another place—from the Greek. But an icon is an image that is worshipped. It's a sacred image.

EF: It is exactly what is worshipped. In the Greek church, the images in the *ikonstatis* are not just pictures of the saints but their actual presence.

SH: But then the Old Testament says, "Thou shalt not make unto thee any graven image. . . . Thou shalt not bow down thyself to them."

EF: But to the believer, the icon is not image but presence.

SH: In this case the icon, Charles, the king, is murdered by those who bowed down to him. He was God's representation on earth. People still believed a king was holy. And this was a culmination of violent deaths on the scaffold in England during the sixteenth century. Raleigh was executed; before him, Sir Thomas More, Mary Queen of Scots, Lady Jane Grey, Essex, just a stream of women and men, powerful ones, religious heretics, biblical translators even, who ended their lives as sacrificial victims. These men and women in power had to be performers. They acted until the moment of death. So executions were staged, but they were real. During the seventeenth century, the masque developed as a sort of political theater where the performers, who were members of the power structure, played other parts. Charles Stuart enjoyed court masques. He performed brilliantly when he was called on to play the victim in his own tragedy. His Puritan accusers also acted brilliantly. Old accounts of the trial are still compelling reading.

Stephen Greenblatt's *Renaissance Self-Fashioning* was a big influence on this poem. And I had in mind Marx's magisterial beginning of *The 18th Brumaire of Louis Bonaparte*. Marx saw the revolutionary situation as theatrical spectacle. And the idea of the dead generations weighing like a nightmare on the brain of the living—the idea of the ghost of the old revolution walking about is so right. The spectacle of the killing of the king accomplished the bourgeois transformation of English society, Marx wrote. It was real, and it was a theatrical event. The ghost is still walking around.

Everything I've been saying comes back to this.

Behind the facade of Harvard University is a scaffold and a regicide. Under the ivy and civility there is the instinct for murder, erasure, and authoritarianism. Behind Milton's beautiful words borrowed from other traditions is a rage to destroy and tear down. He hoped *Eikonoklastes* would erase the *Eikon Basilike* or at least would show it to be a forgery. But *Comus* is a masque and a theatrical performance also. An elaborate facade, a forgery. A poem is an icon.

EF: And so that brings everything around once more to questions about the nature of words. If the icon is not presence—if, as you say in your introduction, "the absent center is the ghost of a king" (by which I understand authority and so the origin of meaning), then what is left in words themselves? What is in the word?

SH: That's it. It's the singularity. It's a catastrophe of bifurcation. There is a sudden leap into another situation. The ghost (the entrance point of a singularity) is the only thing we have. And a ghost represents death. There is death. I almost never put the word *death* in my poems. It would be too easy. I have always felt death to be the unspeakable other.

EF: Perfect absence.

SH: Perfect absence. It's like that part in *Moby-Dick*: "Strike through the mask." What is behind that mask? But you have to strike through it. The mask is the icon. The icon may be a mask. I hope there is something . . . I don't know . . . I mean that's why I am concerned that so much of my work carries violence in it. I don't want to be of Ahab's party. I want to find peace. Anyway, you balance on the edge in poetry. I did say in *My Emily Dickinson* that poetry is dangerous. And I believe this still. But as I go on and on thinking of Emily Dickinson, I think she at last reached a sense of peace—the later letters show it—although the deaths of people close to her probably contributed to her own death; nevertheless, she went to Him—she thought of death as masculine, and so do I—as to a bridegroom. In the end, she betrothed herself to Him.

I think that one reason there is so much ugly antipathy to writers who are breaking form in any way is because people know that language taps an unpredictable power source in all of us. It's not the same in the visual arts, where there are many abstract or form-breaking visual artists who enjoy wide popularity, are embraced by a critical establishment, and sell their work for a tremendous amount of money. You will see their work in museums and books about the work on large glass coffee tables. Try the same thing with language, certainly in this culture, and you may find your writing lost. This is because words are used as buoys, and if they start to break up . . .

EF: If they're stripped of their presumed meanings . . .

SH: Right. Then everything goes because words connect us to life.

EF: Thoreau has an interesting image of the sea surrounding a breakwater or, as he called it, a mole. He calls it a "noble mole," and it's surrounded by the great sea. The great sea is silent, but as the waves wash against and around it, they make sound, and the sound is language.

SH: Well, that's beautiful.

EF: There's silence, and then there's language.

SH: That's true. I don't know why it gets so caught up in fright for me. If you answer the lure of the silence beyond the waves washing, you may enter the sea and drown. It's like Christ's saying if you follow me, you give up your family, you have no family . . . It's following . . . If you follow the word to a certain extent, you may never come back. After all, the mole is put up for protection. But a mole is also a ridge of earth thrown up by moles when burrowing. A mole is a distinguishing mark, a spot or blemish. In Hawthorne's "The Birth-mark," Aylmer kills his wife when he insists on removing the crimson tint on her face. He has grappled with the mystery of life Georgiana's difference represents, and the punishment is her death. A mole was also a cake made of spelt and mixed with salt strewn on the victims at sacrifices. *Mole* is a word tied to the idea of burrowing and excavating. A mole is a spy who spies on spies. The animal is nearly blind. Isn't that beautiful, too—the way the word becomes an infinite chain leading us underground. Words are the only clues we have. What if they fail us?

EF: Well, that's *Moby-Dick*, the chapter with Pip—"The Castaway," isn't it?

SH: Melville—talk about a mole! And Pip burrows or sinks too deep. After writing *Moby-Dick*, where would you be? He wrote *Pierre* almost immediately and then "Bartleby," among other miraculous stories, and then he stopped after *The Confidence Man*. Definitions fall away to nothing in that book. There is absolutely no ground to stand on. It's a trick, a show, a sham, that tells everything. But who could go on in that manner and stay sane? I see why he stopped. Then he wrote poetry, in the sense of verse, for years.

EF: What do you think of it?

SH: I love his Civil War poems. They concern that war, while they could be ancient as the days. But I find *Clarel* hard going. It's one thing I want to carefully read, only other things seem to get in the way. The rhyming puts me off. But I think the discipline he set himself, of making the thing scan and rhyme for volumes, calmed him. The way a chant does in meditation or saying the rosary over and over might do. *Clarel* is how Melville held on. How he kept the sea from rushing over the mole.

EF: His holy land is language.

SH: Well, he did visit the Holy Land, as you know, and his *Journal* is another wonderful thing. *Clarel* was inspired by that visit, but the *Journal* is so immediate. I just found this in it the other day: "Saw a woman over a new grave—no grass on it yet. Such abandonment of misery! Called to the dead, put her head down as close as possible to it; as if calling down a hatchway or a cellar; besought 'Why don't you speak to me? My God—it is I!'. . . —all deaf. So much for consolation.—This woman and her cries haunt me horribly."

The woman is wailing, "My God, it is I," but Melville is saying, "My God, it is I." He is the woman. There is everything in that to me. She's calling to the dead. Who has been buried? Is it her husband, a parent, a child? Melville doesn't know her. He doesn't name her. There is no naming and no answer. She is herself, and he sees himself in her. I think that detail holds everything.

EF: The woman calls only herself.

SH: Of course. "It is I. My God, it is I."

One thing that disturbs me about Olson's attitude toward Melville was his attitude that Melville's Christological pull was some sort of feminine weakness. I think the late work is a going toward peace, like Dickinson, and he had to go that way. Maybe it's just that you build elaborate metaphysical structures when you are young, and when you are older, those structures collapse into something simpler. Fewer words mean more. Ambiguities of history and chronology melt into light in the East. Light, just that.

A subject I would truly love to write on—but I know it's way too much and I never will—is the feminine in Melville. There has to be a reason why his writing speaks so directly to me.

EF: What about Hester Prynne and Hawthorne's . . .

SH: Well, Hawthorne is wonderful, but I think he is a far more sexist writer than Melville. Hawthorne was so crucial for Melville. Then the letters between them. Unfortunately, we only have Melville's side of the correspondence. The missed connections. And the fact that while Hawthorne was writing *The Blithedale Romance*, Melville was writing *Pierre*. Western Massachusetts again. It's the Connecticut River issue again. Emotionally, they were on opposite sides.

EF: Some people want Hawthorne out of the canon or at least on a lower rung since he's said to be sexist.

SH: *The Scarlet Letter* is one of those books I would bring to a desert island. But there is no canon on a desert island anyway.

EF: Well, what about those who say *Moby-Dick* will no longer be read because there are no women in it?

SH: I pity them. It makes me so sad to think that could be said. I feel guilty myself for an attack I made on Olson while I was in Buffalo. And I can see how in some way the feminist issue may do away with interest in Olson by the young. Because Olson is far more extreme than Melville on that subject. If there is Woman in Olson's writing (there aren't women there), she is either "Cunt," "Great Mother," "Cow," or "Whore." But the feminine is very much in his poems in another way, a way similar to Melville. It's voice . . . It has to do with the presence of absence. With articulation of sound forms. The fractured syntax, the gaps, the silences are equal to the sounds in *Maximus*. That's what Butterick saw so clearly. He printed Olson's Space.

I read somewhere that Olson once said that in *Billy Budd*, "the stutter is the plot." There you have Charles Olson at his wisest. "The stutter is the plot." It's the stutter in American literature that interests me. I hear the stutter as a sounding of uncertainty. What is silenced or not quite silenced. All the broken dreams. Thomas Shepard writes them down as soon as 1637. And the rupture from Europe. Continents have entered into contact, creating a zone of catastrophe points. A capture morphology. All that eccentricity. All those cries of "My God, it is I." Mary Rowlandson is an early witness. Metacomet (King Philip) is Leviathan to the Mathers. Rowlandson knows he is human. *Moby-Dick* is a giant stutter in the manner of *Magnalia Christi Americana*. No one has been able to fathom Dickinson's radical representation of matter and radiation—such singularities of space, so many possibilities of choice. History has happened. The narrator is disobedient. A return is necessary, a way for women to go. Because we are in the stutter. We were expelled from the Garden of the Mythology of the American Frontier. The drama's done. We are the wilderness. We have come on to the stage stammering.

Index

Acknowledgments for the use of copyrighted materials:

Reprinted by permission of the publishers from *The Letters of Emily Dickinson*, edited by Thomas H. Johnson, Cambridge, Mass.: The Belknap Press of Harvard University Press, Copyright © 1958, 1986 by the President and Fellows of Harvard College.

Reprinted by permission of the publishers from *The Manuscript Books of Emily Dickinson*, Volumes 1 and 2 edited by R. W. Franklin, Cambridge, Mass.: The Belknap Press of Harvard University Press, Copyright © 1981 by the President and Fellows of Harvard College, Copyright © 1951, 1955, 1978, 1979, 1980, by the President and Fellows of Harvard College, Copyright © 1914, 1924, 1929, 1932, 1935, 1942 by Martha Dickinson Bianchi.

Reprinted with permission of the publishers and the Trustees of Amherst College from *The Poems of Emily Dickinson*, Thomas H. Johnson, ed., Cambridge, Mass.: The Belknap Press of Harvard University Press, Copyright © 1951, 1955, 1979, 1983 by the President and Fellows of Harvard College.

From *Collected Poems* by Wallace Stevens, Copyright © 1942 by Wallace Stevens. Reprinted by permission of the publishers, Alfred A. Knopf, Inc. and Faber and Faber, Ltd.

University Press of New England
publishes books under its own imprint and is the publisher for Brandeis University Press, Brown University Press, University of Connecticut, Dartmouth College, Middlebury College Press, University of New Hampshire, University of Rhode Island, Tufts University, University of Vermont, and Wesleyan University Press.

About the Author

Susan Howe is the author of eleven books of poetry. The daughter of a Harvard Law School professor, Mark DeWolfe Howe, who was also the biographer of Justice Oliver Wendell Holmes, and the Irish playwright and novelist Mary Manning, she graduated from the Boston Museum of Fine Arts in 1961. During the next ten years her work evolved from painting to writing poetry exclusively. At present she is a professor of English at SUNY Buffalo. She has received the Before Columbus Foundation American Book Award twice, in 1980 for *Secret History of the Dividing Line*, and in 1987 for her critical study *My Emily Dickinson*. Howe lives in Guilford, Connecticut, when she isn't teaching in Buffalo.

Library of Congress Cataloging-in-Publication Data
Howe, Susan.
The birth-mark : unsettling the wilderness in American literary history / Susan Howe.
p. cm.
Includes bibliographical references and index.
ISBN 0–8195–5256–9. — ISBN 0–8195–6263–7 (pbk.)
1. American literature—History and criticism—Theory, etc.
2. Dickinson, Emily, 1830–1886—Criticism and interpretation.
3. Rowlandson, Mary White, ca. 1635–ca. 1678. I. Title.
PS25.H68 1993
810.9—dc20 92–56905

∞